T0170125

Understand the Weapon,
Understand the Wound

Collected Writings of John Cornford

RUPERT JOHN CORNFORD (1915–1936) was an English poet, communist and Charles Darwin's great-grandson. He was a member of the International Brigades and died while fighting fascism during the Spanish Civil War. Born in Cambridge, Cornford was educated at Stowe School and Trinity College, Cambridge. As an undergraduate he joined the Communist Party of Great Britain and from 1933 was directly involved in Communist Party work in London. At the start of the Spanish Civil War he briefly served with the P.O.U.M. militia and then with a machine-gun unit of the Commune de Paris Battalion, and fought in defence of Madrid. He was killed in uncertain circumstances at Lopera, near Córdoba, in 1936. A memorial volume to Cornford was published in 1938.

JONATHAN GALASSI is President and Publisher of Farrar, Straus & Giroux in New York City. His novel, *Muse*, was published in 2015.

RICHARD BAXELL is a historian who has written widely about British volunteers in the Spanish Civil War. His latest book, *Unlikely Warriors*, was published by Aurum Press in 2012. He is currently Chair of the International Brigades Memorial Trust.

DR JANE BERNAL is the daughter of Margot Heinemann (1913–1992) and J. D. Bernal (1901–1971). She is currently working on a biography of her mother, to be published by Lawrence & Wishart.

FyfieldBooks aim to make available some of the great classics of British and European literature in clear, affordable formats, and to restore often neglected writers to their place in literary tradition.

FyfieldBooks take their name from the Fyfield elm in Matthew Arnold's 'Scholar Gypsy' and 'Thyrsis'. The tree stood not far from the village where the series was originally devised in 1971.

> *Roam on! The light we sought is shining still.*
> *Dost thou ask proof? Our tree yet crowns the hill,*
> *Our Scholar travels yet the loved hill-side*

from 'Thyrsis'

JOHN CORNFORD

Understand the Weapon, Understand the Wound

Collected Writings

with some letters of Frances Cornford
and afterwords by Richard Baxell and Jane Bernal

edited by
Jonathan Galassi

FyfieldBooks

CARCANET

For Christopher and Lucy Cornford

This revised and expanded edition first published in Great Britain in 2016
by
Carcanet Press Limited
Alliance House
Cross Street
Manchester M2 7AQ
www.carcanet.co.uk

First edition, 1976; second edition, 1989
We welcome your comments on our publications
Write to us at info@carcanet.co.uk

A CIP catalogue record for this book is available from the British Library,
ISBN 9781784102487

The publisher acknowledges financial assistance from Arts Council England

Typeset by XL Publishing Services, Exmouth

Contents

ESSAYS

LETTERS

Notes and Acknowledgements

When possible, the works of John Cornford and of Frances Cornford printed here follow the wording, punctuation and orthography of the extant manuscripts or typescripts, which have been generously made available to the editor by Christopher Cornford. No attempt has been made to correct them. Corrections printed elsewhere have been deleted.

Many of John Cornford's writings originally appeared in *John Cornford: A Memoir*, edited by Pat Sloan (London: Jonathan Cape, 1938). They are reprinted here with the kind permission of the publisher. Thanks are also due to the following for permission to reprint material that originally appeared elsewhere:

Frederick Muller Ltd, for 'Communism in the Universities', first published in *Young Minds for Old: Fourteen Young University Writers on Modern Problems*, edited by Lincoln Ralphs (1936).

Victor Gollancz Ltd, for 'What Communism Stands For', included in *Christianity and the Social Revolution*, edited by John Lewis, Karl Polanyi and Donald K. Kitchin (1935).

Julian Bell's contributions to 'Julian Bell and John Cornford on Art', first published in *The Student Vanguard* for January and March of 1934, are here reprinted with the kind permission of Professor Quentin Bell.

For an understanding of the facts of John Cornford's life I am chiefly indebted to the meticulous scholarship of Peter Stansky and William Abrahams, authors of *Journey to the Frontier; Julian Bell and John Cornford: Their Lives and the 1930s* (London: Constable, 1966).

I would also like to express my personal gratitude to those who have lent me their encouragement, wisdom and support in this project, especially James Atlas, Christopher and Lucy Cornford, Hugh and Jean Cornford, Susan Grace, Margot Heinemann, Helena and Joseph Henderson, James Klugmann and Michael Schmidt.

For this 2016 edition, Richard Baxell and Jane Bernal have contributed incisive afterwords that help us to read John Cornford today. I am grateful to them, and to Adam Cornford and Sandra Mendez Rosenbaum for their tireless efforts to broaden public awareness of Cornford's heroic life and urgent voice.

Chronology

1915   Rupert John Cornford born in Cambridge on 27 December, the second child of Francis Macdonald Cornford (1874–1943), then Lecturer in Classics at Trinity College, and of the poet Frances Crofts Cornford (*née* Darwin) (1886–1960). His sister Helena Darwin Cornford had been born in 1913.

1917   Birth of Christopher Francis Cornford.

1921   Birth of Hugh Wordsworth Cornford.

1924   Birth of Ruth Clare Cornford.

1925   Enters Copthorne School, Sussex.

1929   Enters Stowe School, Buckinghamshire, on 7 October.

1932   Sits scholarship examination for Trinity College, Cambridge in December, winning £100 exhibition.

1933   Enrolls at the London School of Economics in January, where he edits and writes for *The Student Vanguard* and is Secretary of Labour Research Department Study Group on the economics of transport industries. Meets Ray Peters. In October, enters Trinity. Takes part in Armistice Day demonstration 11 November.

1934   Wins First Class Honours, Part I, History Tripos.

1935   Leaves the Young Communist League in March to become a full-fledged member of the Communist Party of Great Britain. Campaigns for Cambridge Labour Party candidate Dr A. Wood, who loses by more than five thousand votes in general election. Chairman, Cambridge University Socialist Society. Contributes 'What Communism Stands For' to *Christianity and the Social Revolution*. Birth of son James, named for fellow Communist James Klugmann. Separation from Ray Peters. Meets Margot Heinemann.

1936   'Communism in the Universities' published in *Young*

Minds for Old. In June, wins B.A. First Class with Distinction in History. Trinity awards him Earl of Derby Research Scholarship. Spanish Civil War breaks out 18 July. Leaves 8 August for Barcelona with letter of introduction from *News Chronicle.* Travels to Saragossa on Aragon front, 11 August. Enlists in P.O.U.M. militia in Lecineña, takes part in attacks on Perdiguera and Huesca. 8–12 September, ill in hospital in Serineña. Returns to Barcelona 13 September. Leaves 14 September to return to England.

Arrives in England 16 September to recruit volunteers for Spain. Resigns scholarships 4 October, leaves for Paris next day with twenty-one Englishmen. To Marseille, then by Anarchist ship to Alicante, and then to Albacete, to join International Brigade. Attached to French Dumont battalion. Battle for Madrid begins 7 November. On the 8th, arrives in Madrid, takes part in battle and attacks on Aravaca and Casa de Campo. 15 November, battle for University City. Wounded by stray anti-aircraft shell, in hospital. Re-assigned to Casa de Campo, elected leader of English.

8 December has relapse, returns to hospital. To Boadilla del Monte 14 December; Fascists force retreat.

By 17 December, five of original twenty-one English remain. Recalled to Albacete to join No. 1 company of English-speaking volunteers in the Marseillaise Battalion of 14th Brigade. Training at Madrigueras. Ordered to Córdoba front.

Leaves Madrigueras 24 December for Andújar and Córdoba front. Reaches ridge above village of Lopera 26 December. Killed in battle 27 or 28 December.

Introduction

Rupert John Cornford died on 27 or 28 December 1936, while fighting with Loyalist forces in a battle for the small village of Lopera on the Córdoba front of the Spanish Civil War. The first Englishman to enlist against Franco, he had gone on, at the age of twenty, to become an acknowledged leader among the British contingent in the International Brigade. Before coming to Spain, as a student at Cambridge he had played an instrumental role in the growth of the Communist movement in British universities, establishing himself at the same time as a potent new force within the Communist Party itself.

His prodigious early achievements and the circumstances of his death have the air of legend about them, and, particularly in the climate of passionate feeling that the Spanish War aroused in Britain and elsewhere, it was natural, perhaps even inevitable, that John Cornford become a hero. His youth and vigour and privileged background, his powerful good looks and intense devotion to his cause, provided all the necessary raw material for the forging of a myth, and as the protagonist of several different sagas, Cornford has served the dramatic needs of a number of ideologies. In one version, he is the romantically dashing reincarnation of his namesake and fellow poet Rupert Brooke, rushing off to Spain in defence of freedom with his father's First World War revolver. To the spectrum of left-liberal opinion convinced of the benignity and inevitability of Communism, before the exposure of the true nature of Stalinism forced them 'to give up all belief in history as the ultimate judge of human affairs', as Hannah Arendt has put it,[1] Cornford embodied the

---

1   In 'Reflections', a memoir of W.H. Auden published in *The New Yorker*, 20 January 1975.

spirit of 'all advanced and progressive mankind'.[2] Still others saw him as '120% Communist', the most dedicated, brilliant and unswerving of Party members, whose death seriously retarded the development of Communism in Britain.

But heroes are larger than life by definition, and less minutely and confusingly drawn than real persons. The legends have purposes of their own; like memory, they tend to distil a multifarious reality into a partial and distorting though coherent whole. We shall never know what John Cornford might have lived to be; but this book brings together his poems, essays and a generous selection of his letters – along with a chronology of his life and some letters from his mother that help to provide a clearer picture of his development – so that the reader may try to construct his own version of what he was, free from the influence of polemical interpretation. These papers provide a sketchy, ragged and probably misleading picture of their author, for a writer always presents himself with some degree of artifice. But they are virtually all we have to tell us how John Cornford saw himself in a variety of private and public postures.

A considerable portion of Cornford's few writings was previously collected in a memorial volume edited by Pat Sloan, which appeared in 1938. But the book has long been out of print; and in many ways it in itself helped to foster the 'liberal' myth about its subject. Out of consideration for others, certain events in Cornford's life went unmentioned, and there were some additional inaccuracies in that winning but somewhat eulogizing composite portrait. Peter Stansky and William Abrahams have contributed a more factually complete record in *Journey to the Frontier*, but they assert in their prologue that 'young men like John Cornford and Julian Bell, both of them poets and sons of the intellectual aristocracy of England [...] were more or less what the legend ['which has tended to overpopulate the Spanish conflict with poets, especially young English poets'] claimed.' 'Heroism, in all its impressiveness

---

2   See the dedication to *John Cornford: A Memoir*, edited by Pat Sloan (London: Cape, 1938).

and absurdity' is what attracts them, and their characterization of Cornford, despite its impeccable reliance on detail, is fundamentally romantic.

The romantic view of John Cornford stems largely from his reputation as a poet; indeed, he is most widely known as a poet of the Spanish Civil War. And it is true that his poems are his most tangible achievement; they are unusually accomplished and powerful, particularly considering the youth of their author. 'These are poems of the will, and the will bangs a drum', Stephen Spender wrote of them.[3] But Cornford composed only three poems in Spain, on his first trip there, and in writing them he seems not to have thought of himself primarily as an artist. When he mentions a desire to write, in a letter from Spain to Margot Heinemann in August 1936 (p. 176), the context implies that he had political, not literary, work in mind.

He had grown up in an extremely rich cultural atmosphere. His father, F.M. Cornford, for whom John felt unwavering respect, was a distinguished scholar of ancient philosophy, and his mother, who was a grand-daughter of Charles Darwin, wrote highly regarded lyrics in the Georgian style. Frances Cornford encouraged her eldest son's early interest in literature, and they exchanged poems and criticism throughout his years at Stowe. John's temperament, however, was radically opposed to hers, and he soon learned to despise her beloved Tennyson and Browning, coming first under the spell of Robert Graves, and somewhat later of Eliot and Auden, all of whose influences can be detected in his poems. Eventually, mother and son found themselves on opposite sides of the unbridgeable chasm of modernism. By 1932, he was writing to her: 'I don't know whether or not I like your poem, or rather whether or not I understand it; because words seem to have a totally different meaning for us' (p. 152). There were other differences, too. In the preceding year or so, John's interests had largely shifted

---

3 Spender published a review of Pat Sloan's *John Cornford: A Memoir*, entitled 'A Communist in Action', in the winter 1938 issue of *Now & Then*.

from literature to politics, and especially to socialism. His younger brother Christopher has written, in an essay for Pat Sloan's book, that 'it was partly through the search for a sociological or historical explanation for the nature of a poem that he came to consider contemporary society, and so politics, and so Communism.' Whatever the causes – and adolescent iconoclasm was probably among them – Cornford's attitude towards his mother's vocation, and her way of life, underwent a profound transformation. That same autumn he also wrote to her: 'I have found it a great relief to stop pretending to be an artist; and in my reaction against overestimating all forms of art for so long I am going through a period of contempt for all artists; which I don't suppose will last long' (p. 147).

Similar overstatements abound in his letters of the period. Nevertheless, from then on poetry was to interest him mainly as a vehicle for reflecting social reality. For a time, his views coincided with those of the younger 'left-wing' English poets; in a letter written to his former schoolmate Tristan Jones shortly before his seventeenth birthday (p. 151) he asks:

> Have you seen Auden's poem 'A Communist to Others', in *Twentieth Century*? It isn't a good poem, but I think it's important, intelligible to every class in the country since about 1580. For the gap between the advanced poets and the public has been growing ever since then.

At Cambridge, where he read history, fathered a child, and was constantly involved in university and adult politics, Cornford continued to write poems intermittently. But even though they were mainly political in theme, and anti-literary in tone (see 'Org. Corn. Discussion on Literature'), he hid them from his Communist friends, and when one, 'Unaware', was published in *The Listener* in 1934, it appeared under a pseudonym. Literary radicalism had lost its attraction for him. Like all serious Marxists of the period, Cornford, according to his roommate and fellow-organizer James Klugmann, came to think that 'Auden was trash'.

From the time he enrolled at the London School of Economics in January 1933, Cornford's writings concentrated almost exclusively on politics. 'Art and the Class Struggle', published in *The Student Vanguard* for May 1933, approaches literature as 'an expression of man [...] in relation to his material surroundings' and finds that 'the best poets of their generation' – Eliot, Joyce, Lawrence – offer only 'collapse and retreat under the stress of decaying capitalism.' 'Left?', written at Cambridge later that year, criticizes the younger generation of English writers, including Spender and Auden, for perpetuating 'the contradiction between art and life, between the life of the artist and the life of society'. According to Cornford, the true revolutionary artist, of which Aragon is an example, is not an 'impartial observer' but an 'objective' participant, bearing witness to the class struggle.

These early polemical pieces on literature and social thought adhere strictly to Communist dogma, and such orthodoxy was to remain broadly characteristic of Cornford's writings as he came to focus on contemporary politics, though, as Jane Bernal points out in her afterword, 'Change and Crisis in the Writings of John Cornford' (p. 195), both the party's views and Cornford's own thinking underwent significant development in these years. The austerity and comprehensiveness of the Marxist analysis of history seem to have completely satisfied his need for a rigorous, organized explanation of the state of society, and for a progressive rationale for action. His later essays strongly emphasize 'correctness' of interpretation, and indicate a wholehearted, if not unquestioning, dedication to both the theoretical 'power of the working class to conquer by direct revolutionary tactics' and the Party's practical application of the theory.

Cornford's analysis of the Spanish War also follows the Party line, although the Communist International's position favoured a coalition with the Republicans and vetoed 'direct revolutionary tactics'. His essay on the war, though written at an earlier stage, offers an interesting counterpoint to Orwell's well-known championing of the Anarchists in *Homage to Catalonia*. Orwell, who was anything but a dogmatist, fought with the

P.O.U.M. (Partido Obrero de Unificación Marxista) under the slogan: 'The war and the revolution are inseparable.' Cornford, in 'The Situation in Catalonia', originally published in *The New Republic*, calls the P.O.U.M. 'parody of the Bolshevik tactics of 1917' dangerous, in that it might drive 'the Republicans into the arms of the reactionaries' (p. 103). 'It is only the unifying force of P.S.U.C. [Partido Socialista Unificado de Cataluña] which can bring republicans, anarchists, police, and civil guards into a unified fighting force' (p. 105) he asserts, with characteristic confidence. The People's Front (whose absence in the Austrian uprising of 1933 he had lamented in 'The Struggle for Power in Western Europe') will ensure 'that the fight to preserve all that is real and valuable in bourgeois democracy in Spain can develop logically, without discord between workers and middle-class Republicans, into a new and higher democracy, a new type of Socialist state machinery.'

'The Situation in Catalonia', like 'What Communism Stands For', demonstrates Cornford's talent for absorbing the Party's positions and disseminating them to a larger public. Elsewhere in these pages, however, we see his dedication to Communism in another light. Writing to Margot Heinemann during his first stint in Spain, he speaks of meeting a group of German ex-members of the Party, who had left it 'because they genuinely felt the C.I. has deserted the revolution' (p. 178). John, at the time still unclear about the Spanish situation, cannot refute their arguments, yet he says, with some rigidity: 'But I am beginning to find out how much the Party and the International have become flesh and blood of me. Even when I can put forward no rational argument, I feel that to cut adrift from the Party is the beginning of political suicide.'

Other anxieties surface, too, most notably in 'Full Moon at Tierz: Before the Storming of Huesca', and in the other poems from Spain, where conflicts between political conviction and personal feeling find striking expression:

Though Communism was my waking time
Always before the lights of home

Shone clear and steady and full in view
Here, if you fall, there's help for you
Now, with my Party, I stand all alone.

Then let my private battle with my nerves,
The fear of pain whose pain survives,
The love that tears me by the roots,
The loneliness that claws my guts,
Fuse in the welded front our fight preserves.

These poems remind us of what we sometimes forget, reading Cornford's essays: that their author is a very young man, facing for the first time the real consequences of his ideas. In them, Cornford struggled to overcome the tradition of the personal, unsocial lyric that he had learned from his mother. But at times the political content of the poems seems at war with their primal emotional motive. For all Cornford's proclamations of international solidarity, they remain the outpourings of a singular character, and what holds us in them finally is their ability to convey the private anguish of that character, testing himself against his vision.

Certainly, Cornford's letters and poems reveal a younger, more pensive, more emotional self than his polemical writings admit. The terror and the loneliness of war stand out vividly between his brave monotone lines. But even in his most dejected moments, the realization that 'Flesh still is weak' is always countered by, or incorporated into, a determination–romantic at root, it may be – to surmount personal and societal obstacles to the goal that his intellectual and moral senses have convinced him is right. At times it may have been only an intense effort of will that maintained him in his course of action. But whatever the reasons, his resolution stayed firm.

This republication of John Cornford's collected writings eighty years after his death celebrates the gem-like intensity of one young man's prodigious desire and need to change the world. There is something universal and immortal about the fierceness of his conviction, through which a young man's doubt shows only rarely. The world in which Cornford became a thinker and a doer at a very early age was in overwhelming political and cultural crisis but his example remains inspiring and exemplary.

Jonathan Galassi
New York City
2016

POEMS

POEMS WRITTEN AT SCHOOL,
[1930]–1932

THIS IS THE WAY THE WORLD ENDS

> We are also gradually tending
> To be less philosophical.
> *R van R G**

[I]

In the beginning the Word, or if you like
In the beginning vast perpetual lakes
Tall rocks, dull marshland drained by squelching dyke
Half riddles. Is man one of God's bad jokes.
And should I ask what came before the rocks
You say innumerable electric sparks
Fusing together with unfeeling shocks –
Earth's wheels slow down – slime interrupted spokes

What came before the sparks? Why, Sir, the Word
Caetera fumus – the very essence of God –
But, Sir, your questionings become absurd
Since all things work together for the best
This problem does not touch us in the least
Leave to your God to order all the rest

Electric sparks: the rocks and sucking mud
Then the first trees of the primeval wood
Apes and then man: and after that the Flood
And why? Because the Lord our God is good
Else say the Word which held the world in girders
Has now outlexiconed its antique warder
The old gods run amuck committing murder.
To answer my next question would be harder

The mask, the painted toughness of the skin
Collapsed, displays the rottenness within
And yesterday, as I walked in the hills
I saw beneath the trawlers shellfished hull
The sagging floors of long dismantled mills
And tend to grow less philosophical.

II *Death of a Hero*

Besieger many years of the inland city
Would let no opportunity slip by,
Now waits the grim speck circling in the sky,
Among black ruins, finding triumph empty.

'Faced with the horrors of a dustbin hell
I tried to storm the citadel within,
To understand myself, which was no sin,
But found no garrison when the fortress fell.

My loud, self conscious skyline operations
Will rob me of the hoped Elysian Field.
I beat at hollow gates with sword and shield,
Claiming to scorn the barbed wire outpost stations.'

Observing carefully this hero's fall,
We know, if ever we attack the city,
We shall abandon antique chivalry
And fight with howitzers or not at all.

MATACHIN

Spoken or written, the word demands a sacrifice:
And we, to remain with its narrow limits,
Must act the parts assigned to us in its myths
Till you, a champion, make legends of your own.

Or shall the symbol of my thought of you
Become the thought, though being itself nothing?

Simplest to act, let us act Philoctetes,
And since the story demands hero and villain
You shall be Philoctetes, guarding the bow,
And I Odysseus, the son of Sisyphus
And not Laertes. We can assign the third part
To whom it fits best when the time comes: and now
Choose our masks, rehearse for the performance.

But the masks provided are not for this play:
Though I can wear the spectators cynic mask
Hardboned, indifferent, taking no part but chorus,
Yet whose is this crumpled image of despair
Unmuscled, limp, this helpless rag of flesh?
And when this is swept away by cold wave, whose is
This falser clearer face outlined beneath?

These are not our masks
Unwounded Philoctetes
Odysseus of no cunning.

These are not our masks
Nor can I discover
Whose is the third part.

Whose is the third who stands always between us
To intercept the thought with empty word?

If we are to act we must act in our own Sagas
Unheroic, avoiding skyline operations.
The older legends have been played through too often.
We must act without masks: for beneath the mask the face
No longer matters: the mind has play through the mask
And is distorted, expressed by borrowed features
Whose static grimace moulds it, plastic, within.

'Hares track curving over the hill through stubble'

Hares track curving over the hill through stubble
Where the sun falls on glittering telegraph wires
And ragged hemlock undergrowth by the stream
Is further evidence of something lost.
(I made this. I have forgotten.)
And by the stream by the willows walking to think
There is something lost, something you cannot recover,
Nor can you remember even what it was.
(I made this. I have forgotten.)
Something in the vision, something so evident
You were unaware of it when sole possessor,
And now its absence troubles the eye, clouds
The finite vision of the bewildering scene.

But this is certain. It is not to be recovered.
No need to recollect, lament, repent,
Regretting what was not enjoyed when had,
Further confusing a confused vision.
Turn back. There is no more peace in this landscape.
Heap up the stubble as fuel for an angry mind
That else will burn what it was lighted to warm.
No peace for you here, no more oneness with earth,
And that is not to be recovered. Turn back.
Go range about the world to gather moss,
An emptier and distracted search. Or remain
Waiting, watching, indifferently observing
Reactions of others or self to useless experiments,
And not revive the apologetic fantasy.
Was it this I who saw more clearly than this?
You can connect previous identity
By scar on the knee, passages of poem remembered,
The face in the mirror unchanged, the single self.
For memory remains. You are the same.
You do not change with different time and place,
But are one actor, playing six parts in a comedy,
Confusing the audience with a single mask.

Huge, empty buildings falling.
(I made this. I have forgotten.)

Shall the eye which saw the land in order
Be blinded by the light which fails without it?
Or will you, at the head of the pass on your alone journey,
Looking back over the green land stretched out beneath you,
Where farms are lighted at evening and smoke goes up straight,
Turn downwards back into that quiet valley?

'To come in darkness to the Maison Dieu'

[1]

To come in darkness to the Maison Dieu
Falling – its silhouette flickers in lightning –
Creates a too well-ordered view of chaos
That hides its ugliness with unfelt symbol –
For superstition gone, here is no more fear –
There is needed a new symbol for chaos.

And this glass door into this ugly house
Whitewashed, with shrubs planted in the sparse earth

Of ragged garden beds,
Its ugliness exceeds all language
Is found no image for this desolation
Heart sinks and mind falls at the prospect
Language is purposeless here, mind's river stagnant.

Better to go in back streets, where ugliness
Is finite to the eye, where rank stench
In nostrils is precise enough for language.
Wall without windows, this house is blind,
A house with no eyes in a back street
Summons the outraged senses to assault.
Here at least is hate, here anger.

2

Follows an introduction of principal characters.
Here the woodcutter, killed at the river Trebia
Leans on his axe to warm himself at fire.
Stir the smouldering embers with your foot, raise
A whirl of sparks to light his passive face. Pass on,
And leave him at his work, who fells the trees
That Hartopp, in elastic sided boots,
And Bleistein, smoking a cigar, burn
On hearths in carpeted rooms.
                              In winter
Rain fell suddenly from indifferent sky
That bogged his tracks and washed away his bridges
He grew no crops, even in drouth had water,
Yet bore the sky no grudge. He observed indifferently
Farmers in village anxiously watching the sky.
This was not his religion, these symbols
Were nothing to him. Himself, he kept
Certain observances, avoiding times of day
Fords and tall trees in country quiet to stranger.
(But you saw him later, before Trebia,
In the same position, warming himself at fire
Awkward in uniform, the straps hurt his shoulders,
Uneasy before battle. Think
He was puzzled and simple, he least of all deserved
This: to be killed later by the river
Struggling with foreign swords and foreign faces
Whose quarrel was not his, who by his death
Gained nothing, not even victory)

'This and this I have learned and taught it myself'

This and this I have learned and taught it myself:
To look from nowhere to expect much good
If to enjoy best what is to be had.
To play a game of chess expertly, studying
The contours of opponents face, observing
From scrutinising eye he too is expert.
And to reduce even this to nothingness
By automatic counters to formal openings.

'This was giants castle, and here was done'

This was giants castle, and here was done
Such and such, magnified and dimmed by legend
Till it means nothing to us. Now these legends
Shall no longer interpose their meaningless language
Between us and the fact.
This land is not worth even the trouble of claiming.
We will disinherit ourselves, and stranger knocking
At the door of this ruined castle must turn back, finding
This is ghosts' house, there is no one to answer the bell.

'There is little left to be done, except to watch'

There is little left to be done, except to watch
Arrival of chaos not of our own making
Nor our preventing. This is a time for destruction.
We fell or fall, but take no part in the building.
What we shall do shall be done for its own sake.
There will be time. There is nothing for us to do
But set down carefully what we have seen or heard
And make this record of ourselves for its own sake also:
Our evidence will be called for at no trial.

'At least to know the sun rising each morning'*

I

At least to know the sun rising each morning
And see at least a sunset's punctual glory
Is at least something. And at least to hear
Water over a rock, all night dripping,
And at least sometimes to walk the mountains all day
On rock above running water. In the winter
Snow falling at least covers the earth, gives promise
Of at least something more than for ever sitting
Here, in darkened rooms frowning back a headache.

Hand on the tiller and the flapping sail,
And brows contracted, the blessing of concentration
On a single time and place, this boat, this sail.
Wind in the roots of the hair, eyes see no further
Than the small circles of the rain downwards falling
Silently into the sea, and far enough.

II

Leave off loving and be hating:
Complete the final well-worn round.
Practised in all the arts of hurting
Satisfy the will to wound.

Whirled by wind the cold sleet falling
Smoulders rage, hinders its stroke.
But even now, with anger falling,
Exploit your mood for its own sake.

Carry your hatred to its limit,
Expose to wind and sleet those sores,

And when exhaustion comes to end it
With no pride show healing scars.

III

Here snow was
Falling apparently from open sky.
Wind marks the clear-cut cheekbone. Emptiness and coldness
That were our skyline were for us gladness.

Passing from here to residential suburb,
And later to the centre of a big city,
Was a transition thought not easy
But made with nothing worse than a headache.

At the street corners they were selling papers,
Told us what teeth were broken in what riots,
Where fighting on the frontier is unsuccessful
But causes as yet no panic in the city.
Think. Rome fell not otherwise from this
Who, dying slowly, is spared defeat,
Suffers, perhaps, greater humiliation.
Here lights and wine, here meeting by chance a friend
Who at my elbow during hour of crisis
Directed operations, staved off breakdown.

Answers to questions: is transition easy?
I was by now accustomed to unreason,
Nor were you puzzled, searching for a oneness.

IV

I am beginning again, did I tell you?
I can no longer drag these dead emotions
Out of a wearied mind that feels them differently

Or not at all. Firstly I must dispose of
The text books for the conduct of operations
I carried with me. You and you my masters,
Though you have told me exactly what to do
Are now no longer wanted, I cannot bother
To imitate your actions nor your heroes.
I have no longer need to borrow your spectacles.
I am coming to see for myself, and stranger knocking
At the door of my former castle, must turn back, finding
This is ghosts' house, there is no one to answer the bell.

'Living in tomorrow or perhaps yesterday'

Living in tomorrow or perhaps yesterday
Or perhaps not in time, but not today
Here there were only three days in the week
And twenty minutes were a full hour
But should they watch the clock, hands were still
And time thus stopped was still wasted
Yet hands moved rapidly when they were absent
Irregularly ticked to their fever –
We must do something, there is nothing to be done.
Crumbling, crumbled to powder: dust from carpets
Settled down silently on their inaction.

(And their repeated unanswered question: shall we
Bring new keels to our dockyard, shall we
Cut a fresh channel through silted harbourmouth?
Is it too late for such and such a revival?)

Facing each way to face disaster was tension. Signs
Were wonders in this brittled atmosphere
Here one smiled, here another frowned
Or snow fell suddenly from cloudless sky:
Symbols became portents of coming disaster
By signs they half remembered

What had not been yet. At this point, they said,
Here where we are past and future cross. Till each made,
For himself, phantasies of these portents, which
Became his sole reality, till
The time in them became the actual time,
Memory failed, and the dead walked.
And they, who had faced disaster at compass points,
Had not foreseen this inner chaos. Disaster
Struck from within and smashed outer defences.

FOR ELISABETH*

Cowbells and running water in the mountains
And coming over into quiet country,
Stumbling, leaping downhill, too tired to walk –
Lips bilberry-stained that once kissed yours.
Now once again is pleasure in solid objects,
Boots treading the path and lights in the village at evening.

And it is best so to invert time,
So that the memory of one hot, close night
And happiness in the slow sound of your breathing
Is further and less fevered, though unforgotten.

And come again to you simply, assuming forgiveness
For how I have wronged you and wronged myself,
Once shattered but calmer now, though something is lost.
And have prepared no sweated, unnatural gesture –
Ronsard me célébrait, but without conviction –
And see you as you are, now the false colours
Of hope and lust through which I once saw your picture
In my mind, are faded, no more mislead my vision.
Into a quiet valley in the cool of the evening
Once more beside you. Now no longer see me
As I once wished you to, but as I am.

POEMS WRITTEN AT CAMBRIDGE, 1933–1936

'All this half-felt sorrow and all this unfelt laughter'

All this half-felt sorrow and all this unfelt laughter
Is the question to be decided, and I am the answer.
Wherever the vague sea wanders in the blind cold useless dark
It shatters itself on the coastline, my purpose, heavy as rock.
How much must we hurt each other before you let yourself know
What my strength and your misfortune decided long ago?

'Should spring bring remembrance, a raw wound smarting?'

Should spring bring remembrance, a raw wound smarting?
Say rather for us fine weather for hurting,
    For there's no parting curse we fear.
Here we break for good with the old way of living,
For we're leaving only what wasn't worth having,
    And face turned forward, for there's no life here.

Best cut out all the talk of renewing
And wordy philosophies of destroying –
    Easiest far to tell them straight
We don't do this for fun, and, joking apart
We mean what we say, and don't care if we hurt,
    For there's plenty to do, and no time to wait.

Who know the future holds pain and anger
Need pay no heed to their warnings of danger;
    Better to drink too deeply than not at all.
'If you move too hastily you'll regret it,
And when we were where you are, we didn't forget it.'
    Exactly – and it's you that's going to fall.

Though you don't like our looks, or the way we behave,
Or the way we think, or the way we love,
    You'd better realise you've made a mistake,
If you think you can shake us with the charge of betrayal,
For we're not ashamed of being disloyal
    To compulsion – contracts that we didn't make.

Now we've slipped your bandage from over our eyes,
And can see as surrender what you called compromise.
    We're ready for all you thought caddish to do;
Throw pepper in the eyes of the policeman's horses,
Seduce from allegiance His Majesties forces,
    And finish as victors, when you're in the zoo.

You know at what forge our purpose was steeled,
At what anvil was hammered the hammer we wield,
    Who cut the sickle to a cutting edge.
And under the light of our five-point star
The faces you see here are different far
    From those at the closed works, or fallen bridge.

The sky is darkening with great clouds,
And from the cold north the sullen crowds'
    Songs startle the streets of the derelict town.
'No more they're deceived by their leaders mock strife,
In action demanding for all bread and life,
    For all bread and life' – and the storm sweeps down.

Not the dreamed-of battle on the windy plain,
But light slitting the eyelids in the cold dawn,
    The old world seen in a new light.
And see! the fist of the silent defender
Is clenched to strike as we gather under
    Our banner 'Students and Workers Unite!'

Now the crazy structure of the old worlds reeling,
They can see with their own eyes its pitprops falling,

Whether they like it, or whether they don't.
Though they lie to themselves so as not to discover
That their game is up, that their day is over,
  They can't be deaf to our shout 'RED FRONT!'

'This is the slackened tempo of defeat'

This is the slackened tempo of defeat
Summer is limp and sweating as unclenched fists
You can't melt metal by sun's straight heat,
And this year of all is no year to retreat
But we were disorganized by the first arrest.

And thunder now would lift the weight
Of summer from our minds. This dust needs rain
But weather won't make our enemies wait
We shall have to get used to harder things than heat.
Tension is all. We have a world to win.

ORG. COM. DISCUSSION ON LITERATURE*

Wind from the dead land, hollow men,
Webster's skull and Eliot's pen,
The important words that come between
The unhappy eye and the difficult scene.
All the obscure important names
For silly griefs and silly shames,
All the tricks we once thought smart,
The kestrel joy and the change of heart,
The dark mysterious urge of the blood
The donkeys shitting on Dali's food,
There's none of these fashions have come to stay
And there's nobody here got time to play.
All we've brought are our party cards
Which are no bloody good for your bloody charades.

UNAWARE*

They keep their nerve on ledges still
And climbing granite wail
Carry no fear
Of lightning's stroke on face of rock
Or depthless falling

Homing at evening tired after sailing
Beyond boats' foamwide wake
Eyes unsurprised
See over dunes first sign of rains
And skyline blacken

Yet eyes' clearness brings no awareness
And compromised with fate
They'll hear in fear
The clock's strict time tick out their doom
Who had fallen better

AS OUR MIGHT LESSENS*

Mind shall be harder
Heart the keener
Mood the more
As our might lessens.

1

These carrion men that fear our power,
The heroes of the pogrom hour,
Who measure virtue by the strength to kill,
Because they know their time is near,
Would hold us down by murder's fear.
The dying crucify the living still.

For those whose tortured torturing flesh
Stirred at the body under the lash,
The painted boy in the praetorians bed.
For those who were strong to love and live,
Who claimed life had no need to starve,
Camphor and pincers fouled urine and blood.

Our girls whose limbs were shaped for love,
But love as equal not as slave,
Were raped by madmen on the wooden horse,
Who dying fought life's weakness down
Our men, castrated, still were men,
For manhood in their living burnt so fierce.

For all but suicides and slaves
This death is background to our lives,
This is the risk our freedom has us take.
Some may die bold as Schulze died,
Many will live to avenge our dead,
But this fear haunts us all. Flesh still is weak.

2

No abstraction of the brain
Will counteract the animal pain.
The living thought must put on flesh and blood.
Action intervenes, revealing
New ways of love, new ways of feeling,
Gives nerve and bone and muscle to the word.

Action creates new ways of living,
Shatters the old ideas of loving,
Brings us in motion face to face with fact.
In forcing us to readjust
The half-adjustments of the past
Strips all illusions from the sexual act.

Locked in the first or final kiss,
No time for thought, you know that this
In ebb or flow of movement will keep steady.
Feeling love's wanton buttocks move,
Scaling your sex, you know all life,
All strength moves in the dance of a woman's body.

Only the maimed talk of soul's dress.
Her glory is her nakedness,
The free surrender fusing love and lust.
And manhood muscled by this love
Under the madman's whip can prove
Stronger than the force by which its life was crushed.

Even now while we have yet to win
Our light from dark, our senses can
Oppose this burning life to that charred by death.
Love gives a new, a stranger pride,
And we go taller by a head,
Now nerve and senses check the compassed path.

3

We cannot hope to ease life's itch
Gleaning the harvest of the rich,
Gathering the rotten peaches from the trees.
And by retreating to the mind,
However deep we grub, we'll find
No magic formulae, no golden keys.

Not by any introspection
Can we regain the name of action.
Whatever dreams may mean to you, they mean sleep.
Black over Europe falls the night,
The darkness of our long retreat,
And winter closes with a silent grip.

But what the dawn will bring to light,
Victory or fresh defeat,
Depends on us until the nightmare's over.
On how we fight their truth and lies,
Their death in rescuer's disguise,
Till the ice starts breaking up on the frozen river.

Though flesh is weak, though bone is brittle,
Our sinews must be hard as metal.
We must learn to mock at what makes readers wince.
Our home, our job is everywhere,
We have no time to stand and stare,
Nor miss the fighter's nor the lover's chance.

We cannot hide from life with thought,
And freedom must be won, not bought.
No talisman will keep us safe from harm.
But moving in the masses blood
Vienna, Amsterdam, Madrid
The ten-years-sleeping image of the storm

Shows us what we stand to gain,
If through this senseless-seeming pain,
If through this hell we keep our nerve and pride
Where the nightmare faces grinned
We, or our sons, shall wake to find
A naked girl, the future at our side.

4

No poets conjuring lotus words,
No images of flowers and birds
Can bring from dream his eunuch's fairyland,
And only those who fear the light
Crouch and worship at the feet
Of the blind goddess born in dark of mind.

Not force, nor flattery, nor lie,
Nor law can win, nor money buy
A girl's surrender for the dispossessed.
But yet the freedom of our hate,
The equal sorrow of the night
Of anger clenched within the shutting fist

Can free her from the ancient lies,
The artificial mysteries
That changed her weakness into poison's power,
And love brings comfort to the bed
Of the outcast disinherited,
Warming the frozen limbs till zero-hour.

*SERGEI MIRONOVITCH KIROV**

Nothing is ever certain, nothing is ever safe,
To-day is overturning yesterday's settled good.
Everything dying keeps a hungry grip on life.
Nothing is ever born without screaming and blood.

Understand the weapon, understand the wound:
What shapeless past was hammered to action by his deeds,
Only in constant action was his constant certainty found.
He will throw a longer shadow as time recedes.

SAD POEM

I loved you with all that was in me, hard and blind,
Strove to possess all that my arms could bind,
Only in your loving found my peace of mind.
But something is broken, something is gone,
We've loved each other too long to try to be kind,
This will turn to falseness if it goes on.

Though parting's as cruel as the surgeon's knife,
It's better than the ingrown canker, the rotten leaf.
All that I know is I have got to leave.
There's new life fighting in me to get at the air,
And I can't stop its mouth with the rags of old love.
Clean wounds are easiest to bear.

Else feel the warm response grow each night colder,
The fires of our strength in each other ash and smoulder.
Nothing that we do can prevent that we have grown older,
No words to say, no tears to weep.
Don't think any more, dear, rest your dark head on my shoulder,
And try to sleep, now, try to sleep.

*A HAPPY NEW YEAR**

All last night we lay so close,
All completeness of the heart
The restless future will efface –
Tomorrow night we sleep apart.

The eyeless shutter clamping out,
Dear, the certainty of your touch;
All the warmth and all the light –
Oh don't think, it hurts too much.

Though your nerves are frozen numb
Your sorrow will not make time stop,
You're not a statue but a man;
Oh don't grieve, it doesn't help.

POEMS FROM SPAIN, 1936

FULL MOON AT TIERZ:
*BEFORE THE STORMING OF HUESCA**

1

The past, a glacier, gripped the mountain wall,
And time was inches, dark was all.
But here it scales the end of the range,
The dialectic's point of change,
Crashes in light and minutes to its fall.

Time present is a cataract whose force
Breaks down the banks even at its source
And history forming in our hand's
Not plasticine but roaring sands,
Yet we must swing it to its final course.

The intersecting lines that cross both ways,
Time future, has no image in space,
Crooked as the road that we must tread,
Straight as our bullets fly ahead.
We are the future. The last fight let us face.

2

Where, in the fields by Huesca, the full moon
Throws shadows clear as daylight's, soon
The innocence of this quiet plain
Will fade in sweat and blood, in pain,
As our decisive hold is lost or won.

All round the barren hills of Aragon
Announce our testing has begun.
Here what the Seventh Congress said,
If true, if false, is live or dead,
Speaks in the Oviedo mausers tone.

Three years ago Dimitrov fought alone
And we stood taller when he won.
But now the Leipzig dragon's teeth
Sprout strong and handsome against death
And here an army fights where there was one.

We studied well how to begin this fight,
Our Maurice Thorez held the light.
But now by Monte Aragon
We plunge into the dark alone,
Earth's newest planet wheeling through the night.

3

Though Communism was my waking time,
Always before the lights of home
Shone clear and steady and full in view –
Here, if you fall, there's help for you –
Now, with my Party, I stand quite alone.

Then let my private battle with my nerves,
The fear of pain whose pain survives,
The love that tears me by the roots,
The loneliness that claws my guts,
Fuse in the welded front our fight preserves.

O be invincible as the strong sun,
Hard as the metal of my gun,
O let the mounting tempo of the train
Sweep where my footsteps slipped in vain,
October in the rhythm of its run.

4

Now the same night falls over Germany
And the impartial beauty of the stars
Lights from the unfeeling sky
Oranienburg and freedom's crooked scars.
We can do nothing to ease that pain
But prove the agony was not in vain.

England is silent under the same moon,
From Clydeside to the gutted pits of Wales.
The innocent mask conceals that soon
Here, too, our freedom's swaying in the scales.
O understand before too late
Freedom was never held without a fight.

Freedom is an easily spoken word
But facts are stubborn things. Here, too, in Spain
Our fight's not won till the workers of all the world
Stand by our guard on Huesca's plain
Swear that our dead fought not in vain,
Raise the red flag triumphantly
For Communism and for liberty.

[TO MARGOT HEINEMANN]*

Heart of the heartless world,
Dear heart, the thought of you
Is the pain at my side,
The shadow that chills my view.

The wind rises in the evening,
Reminds that autumn's near.
I am afraid to lose you,
I am afraid of my fear.

On the last mile to Huesca,
The last fence for our pride,
Think so kindly, dear, that I
Sense you at my side.

And if bad luck should lay my strength
Into the shallow grave,
Remember all the good you can;
Don't forget my love.

*A LETTER FROM ARAGON**

This is a quiet sector of a quiet front.

We buried Ruiz in a new pine coffin,
But the shroud was too small and his washed feet stuck out.
The stink of his corpse came through the clean pine boards
And some of the bearers wrapped handkerchiefs round their
faces.
Death was not dignified.
We hacked a ragged grave in the unfriendly earth
And fired a ragged volley over the grave.

You could tell from our listlessness, no one much missed him.

This is a quiet sector of a quiet front.
There is no poison gas and no H. E.*

But when they shelled the other end of the village
And the streets were choked with dust
Women came screaming out of the crumbling houses,
Clutched under one arm the naked rump of an infant.
I thought: how ugly fear is.

This is a quiet sector of a quiet front.
Our nerves are steady; we all sleep soundly.

In the clean hospital bed, my eyes were so heavy
Sleep easily blotted out one ugly picture,
A wounded militiaman moaning on a stretcher,
Now out of danger, but still crying for water,
Strong against death, but unprepared for such pain.

This on a quiet front.

But when I shook hands to leave, an Anarchist worker
Said: 'Tell the workers of England
This was a war not of our own making
We did not seek it.
But if ever the Fascists again rule Barcelona
It will be as a heap of ruins with us workers beneath it.'

ESSAYS

STUDENTS – NOT SCABS*

During the general strike of 1926 it was taken for granted by the University authorities and the ruling class as a whole that the students could be relied upon to act in a solid mass as scabs and strikebreakers. And they were not disappointed. The lack of any active organisation among those students who were conscious of the real issues of the strike enabled the authorities to exploit to the full the indifference and the lack of political consciousness of the mass of students, and they made full use of their opportunity. The result was that the students rallied in a solid mass to break a strike of whose causes and significance they were ignorant, and under such circumstances that the real issues involved were consciously obscured and distorted by the vilest reactionary propaganda. And more than this. Certain individual students who wished to take the side of the strikers were forbidden to do so by their college authorities.

In 1933, we are faced with a very different situation. The very rapid growth of political consciousness has led many more of the students to realise with which class their real interests lie. Recently we had a striking example of the change in the position. Whereas in 1926 the authorities had been able to appeal for strikebreakers, in the Irish rail strike of this year the Queen's University, Belfast, Union was compelled to issue a formal declaration of non-responsibility for the scabbing of individual students – and it was compelled to issue this declaration largely as the result of the forcible expression of student opinion in resolutions that were sent to Belfast from all over Britain. Reaction is on the defensive.

But this shows an important shift in the correlation of forces, it does not in itself constitute a victory. To pass resolutions is not enough. The only valid test of our success in securing an organised expression of student opinion is that of action; and unless we can do something more than pass resolutions, we will not pass this test. We are faced this year with the imminent prospect of a transport strike in London, and the probability of a nation-wide rail strike, as well as a number of local strikes, like that at Dagenham.

The fight against student scabbing, however, does not begin from the time of declaration of the strike. It begins now. For it is not an isolated question of political opinion. It is directly connected with the fight against reaction, against Fascism, against education cuts, against war.

In a strike situation, of course, our work will consist of a great deal more than this. We shall have to explain and popularise the aims of the strike as widely as possible. We shall have to prevent scabbing by any means in our power, from peaceful dissuasion to picketing in force. And we shall put our services, as individuals or as organised bodies, at the disposal of the strike committees for whatever purpose they are most needed. But until then, any broadening and deepening of political consciousness over any issue further strengthens the fight against reaction in general and student scabbing in particular.

ART AND THE CLASS-STRUGGLE:
A REPLY TO RAYNER HEPPENSTALL *

AN important feature of the decay of capitalism, as reflected in the art it produces, is the separation of art from experience, the flight of the artist from reality. Among the significant artists of to-day there are several varieties of such a retreat. The retreat behind a barrier of obsolete cultural and religious values and prejudices – T. S. Eliot. The retreat into idealised historical phantasies about a world that never did nor could exist – Richard Aldington, Ezra Pound. The retreat towards a more simple and primitive form of civilisation – D. H. Lawrence. The disintegration of a superb technical talent into a paranoiac persecution-and-conspiracy phantasy – Wyndham Lewis. The retreat of James Joyce is so skilfully covered by a barrage of unintelligibility (or meaninglessness?) that it is only possible to say with confidence that, wherever it leads, it leads away from objective reality.

Art like any other expression of man, such as science and politics, cannot be divorced from reality, i.e., from man in relation to his material surroundings. The idea of a detached, impartial artist is therefore utterly false. The class struggle is a conflict between the dynamic force of revolution and what Engels called the 'inertia force of history.' Any 'detachment' from this conflict means siding with the inertia force. In so far as he attempts to isolate T. S. Eliot's poetry from his criticism, Rayner Heppenstall subscribes to the myth of the detached artist, and it is here that his analysis of Eliot is at fault.

Once this is perfectly clear, that flight from reality by the writers I have already mentioned is not difficult to explain. It is due first of all to a loathing for the outward manifestations of a decaying social order, and secondly to an inability or unwillingness to appreciate correctly the forces at work beneath the surface that have produced these manifestations. All of them have indulged in violent satire of these outward symptoms; not a single one of them has even hinted at a cure for the sick society whose diseases they so convincingly describe. Consequently they either adopt a defeatist attitude, or else they simply close their eyes and keep them tight shut. It is not so much because they are frightened of Communism, as because they are one and all unable to see the forces at work beneath the surface in their correct perspective.

The Waste Land is the most typical poem of that generation of writers. It is of great importance, not for the pleasure it gives, but for its perfect picture of the disintegration of a civilisation. Its second section, as a picture of the two classes, could hardly be bettered. But something more than description, some analysis of the situation is needed. And it is here that Eliot breaks down. He refuses to answer the question he has so perfectly formulated. He retreats into the familiar triangle – Classicism, Royalism, Anglo-Catholicism. He has not found an answer to the question in resignation. Rather he has resigned himself to finding no answer.

Or take the case of Lawrence. He, as proletarian-born himself, comes closer to an analysis. The theme of almost all his novels is the vertical invasion of the proletariat, smashing upwards through all class-distinctions to regenerate society – expressed, of course, in terms of individual relationships. But he was objectively unable to grasp the concept that he gave such an admirable subjective formulation. Consequently he too fell into a defeatist attitude, and spent the last few years of his life travelling all over the world in search of the ideal primitive community, which, of course, he never found nor could have found.

The case of Joyce is much the same as Eliot's. *Ulysses* is a less formally perfect, less integrated version of the content of *The Waste Land;* Joyce's retreat, too, is on the same lines as Eliot's, but more precipitate and less dignified. Pound's Provencal phantasies and Aldington's verse short-story, *A Dream in the Luxembourg*, tell exactly the same story of a pathetic escape from a reality they were unable to analyse. Lewis is the only one who makes any attempt to analyse the situation in objective terms. But he is so subjectively orientated, so isolated from the historic process, that any grain of truth that he may grasp, when applied to concrete realities, is ludicrously distorted.

These, then, are the best poets of their generation; and all they have to offer is collapse and retreat under the stress of decaying capitalism.

THE CLASS FRONT OF MODERN ART*

THE period of bourgeois decline in the epoch of Imperialism, marked by the end of the possibility of the outward expansion of capitalism when the whole of the earth has been divided into colonies and markets, is marked by a corresponding change of position on the ideological front. The old 'progressive' materialism which served the bourgeoisie in its struggle against reactionary feudal mysticism, is abandoned in favour of a no less reactionary idealism. Economic theories of Free Trade and Free Competition are replaced by the fascist doctrine of 'national self-sufficiency.'

Psychology is more and more openly used as a class weapon – in its 'practical' form (industrial psychology) as a means of reconciling factory workers and employees to their environment in order to prevent their rebelling against it; in its more mystical forms as a new brand of opium for the people, a religion-substitute for the petty-bourgeoisie; in its more highly-developed theoretical forms as an idealist counter-attack against the historical materialist analysis of society. So also with art. This too is no longer a dynamic cultural force, but is as much a check on the cultural development of society as the bourgeois property-relations are on its productive development.

Contradictions

The characteristic feature of the decay of bourgeois art is the recurring concept of the contradiction between art and life. This can be traced in different forms in the work of all the leading writers. Perhaps its most conscious formulation by a poet is W. B. Yeats': 'The intellectual man is forced to choose / Perfection of the art or of the life' [*sic*]. And it occurs in the romantic concept of poetry as an escape from life, as in Stephen Spender's: 'The city builds its horror in my brain, / This writing is my only wings away.' And in a highly significant passage in *The Sacred Wood*, T. S. Eliot states that literary experience is of the same validity and can be considered on the same level as other direct forms of experience, which is a more positive formulation of the same basic idea. And even where it has no conscious formulation, the same concept can be found running through the work of the leading bourgeois writers, not as a theoretical concept but as an unchallenged axiom. Ezra Pound's idealist-romantic historical poems – which are complementary to the violent but petty and *unhistorical* contemporary satires, show just the same tendency. For Pound approaches his medieval Provence through its literature and not through its history. It is an escape into the literature of the past to avoid the present reality. His criterion for the judgment of the world to-day is a previous epoch's judgment of itself.

The Artist in Society

And from the concept of the contradiction between art and life arises as the next logical step the idea of the contradiction of the life of the artist with the life of society. The fictionised autobiography of Rainer Maria Rilke, the German poet, *The Notebooks of Malte Laurids Brigge*, is the classic example of this. The hero is portrayed as hypersensitive to the verge of insanity, driven almost crazy by continual neurotic introspection, sinking frequently into a wearingly abject self-pity. The life and work of the French novelist, Proust, show exactly the same super-subjectivity. Perhaps the most detailed formulation of the contradiction between the life of the artist and the life of society is Hermann Hesse's novel *Steppenwolf*, which is devoted exclusively to the subject. It is a very interesting book, because Hesse comes closer than any of the others to understanding the objective causes for this contradiction. He specifically states that whilst the Steppenwolf (who represents the bourgeois writer) is antagonistic to the form of society in which he finds himself, his attempts to alter it are confined to criticism in his writings, usually from a subjective standpoint; he cannot take up a more active struggle against it *because he is ultimately dependent on it.* Exactly the same idea is the main theme of a novel by Thomas Mann, *Tonio Kroeger.*

This seeming antagonism to bourgeois society is not in any sense revolutionary. D. H. Lawrence condemned (in words) the bourgeois; but he found the Bolshevik equally detestable. And this is equally true of his contemporaries. His disciple, Richard Aldington, writes lyrical hymns of hate against the bourgeoisie: but also thinks that the class war is 'poisonous bunk.' For the idea of the contradiction between art and life is complementary to the idea of the artist as a lofty and impartial observer, standing above the petty conflicts of society. By this disguise of impartiality they attempt to conceal the fact, more honestly recognised by Hermann Hesse, that they are inactive because they have not sufficiently the courage of their convictions to be renegades to their class – with all its unpleasant and dangerous social consequences. When Louis Aragon, one of the members of the Surréaliste group, went over to the Communists and was imprisoned on the charge of incitement for his poem *The Red Front*, he was quickly enough abandoned by the rest of the group.

For those who realise that the class conflict in society is a struggle between the dynamic and vital forces of society against the reactionary inertial forces, the idea of the 'impartial' artist is an absurdity. To stand outside the conflict is to add to the deadweight of the forces of reaction and inertia. Thus the seeming antagonism between the bourgeoisie and its artists serves only to conceal that their class interests are fundamentally the same – incidentally serving a very useful political purpose in diverting the potentially revolutionary forces among the bourgeois intellectuals into safe literary channels.

Art and Fascism

But in its final stage of crisis when the bourgeoisie is forced to abandon its veiled 'democratic' form of dictatorship in favour of its openly terrorist fascist dictatorship, all art and all science, however far they are separated by class-prejudice from an objective dialectical attitude, must be suppressed because they are potentially dangerous. It is not an exaggeration to state that fascist Italy and Germany have expelled or silenced practically every artist or scientist of any ability. The bankruptcy of the official fascist artists is so pitiful that an increasing section of the intellectuals of both countries realises more and more clearly the class-issues involved and goes over to the revolution. But in those countries where the transition to fascism through the 'democratic' state machinery is still taking place, where the simple class issue has not been presented in as brutally direct form as it was presented to the Italians and Germans, a further change of front is taking place among the bourgeois artists, an attempted adaptation to the new policy of the bourgeoisie. Ezra Pound leads the way, coming out as an open fascist and at the same time a simpleminded propagandist for Douglas credit. Wyndham Lewis two years ago wrote a book about Hitler, containing a lame apology for his anti-semitism, and the curious theory that Hitler is a man of peace because he is the 'German man.' Since Lewis appears to have relied exclusively on the Nazi press and propaganda for information about the movement, the book appears now utterly grotesque. Nevertheless it represents a significant ideological tendency. T. S. Eliot also follows rather hesitatingly. When taken in conjunction with the preface to E. A. Mowrer's book in America, with its elevation of racial theory, the anti-semitic passages in *Burbank*, and *Bleistein* and *Gerontion* have more than a passing significance. But this is not a process of adaptation that will ever have time to complete itself. The historical process does not greatly concern itself with the subjective reaction of individuals to it; and it will not stand still and wait while these gentlemen attempt to define their relation to it.

Meanwhile, all over the world there is growing up a revolutionary movement in literature which flatly denies that there is a contradiction between art and life, which rejects the theory of artistic 'impartiality.' Its writers do not regard themselves as isolated and detached observers of history, but as active participators. Their work is born out of struggle. Ernst Toller, the workers' councillor of the Bavarian Soviet, who was forced to escape with a price of 10,000 marks on his head, wrote his first plays secretly in prison. Theodor Plivier, the novelist of the revolt in the German navy, took an active part as an able seaman in the events he describes. Pudovkin and Eisenstein, whose films *The End of St. Petersburg* and *Battleship Potemkin* mark the peak of revolutionary art, both took part in the revolution. And these are only a few examples of a universal movement. Everywhere a revolutionary literature is being written with a crude and violent energy comparable only to the force of the earlier artists of the bourgeois revolution, men such as Kyd and Marlowe; but with this difference, that the hero is no longer the great king or successful general, but the working class as a whole.

In England the movement is not as advanced as elsewhere, but the same stirrings can be found in some of the work of the younger poets, Auden, Madge and a few others. And although the very youth of these writers, and their consequent inexperience of the revolutionary movement, means that the work still has largely the content of a literary revolt against the concept of the contradiction between art and life, the only possible logical development is towards a consistently revolutionary standpoint.

In the course of its development some of its members will leave it when it becomes clear that it offers little future for a bourgeois literary career (just as the Surréalistes left Aragon), and some will lag behind the tempo of events and become mere 'fellow-travellers' with the movement. But it is not our business here to decide what part the various individuals will play in its development. It is sufficient to know that only from this quarter can come a successful struggle for free development of culture against the cultural reaction.

*JULIAN BELL AND JOHN CORNFORD ON ART**

The Editor, STUDENT VANGUARD.

Sir,

Surely John Cornford has something better to give us in the way of a Marxist analysis of the present poetic situation than this attempt to impose Middleton Murry's aesthetic absolutism under the disguise of a contradiction. To suppose that you can use 'dynamic' and 'static' as equivalents for 'good' and 'bad,' or that you can equate 'dynamic' with 'revolutionary' and 'static' with 'reactionary,' is simply a grotesque piece of false over-simplification and verbal indefiniteness. In what sense is Toller more dynamic than D. H. Lawrence? 'Dynamic' is exactly the sort of vague bad language beloved of fascists and mystics; Hitler and Mussolini are both thoroughly 'dynamic.' Cornford seems to be very far from clear as to the part to be played by contemporary poets in the revolutionary movement. I would suggest, as a tentative analysis, that poets, as such, have very little part to play in the movement. Whatever their class origins, anyone who acquires enough literary training and practice to be able to write poetry at all becomes involved in the

European literary tradition. That is, he becomes interested in his own emotions, and looks to the arts as a form of self-expression. And he finds ready to hand a highly developed technique for expressing his more personal and intimate emotions. Naturally, writers like Auden are only able to write about what it feels like to be a bourgeois intellectual who is politically on the left. And writers like D. H. Lawrence are only able to write about what it feels like to be an educated proletarian. For it is no good hoping to extricate oneself from a historical process by the simple expedient of going over to the other side. Everyone, bourgeois or proletarian, has to-day the kind of mind produced by the historical development of capitalism. We might go on to prophesy that a revolutionary situation will modify the existing poetic tradition – probably by extinguishing the poets – and that the poetry of a classless state will be like either the poetry of revolting bourgeois or of revolting proletarians; that it will be a poetry produced by a stable, not a revolutionary environment. Consequently, we should recognise modern revolutionary poetry as being definitely contemporary and ephemeral. Its chances of 'immortality' – of being read in five hundred years' time – are no better than the chances of reactionary poets like Yeats or Eliot. 'Immortality' depends on the writers being able to use language in such a way as to arouse some of the highly-valued emotions which are comparatively stable in changed environments.

By insisting on the badness of 'artistic impartiality,' Cornford seems to confuse yet further the position of the left intellectual. It is certainly desirable that anyone with abilities for doing so should take part in the revolutionary movement, but it is highly improbable that anyone who does so will have time and energy enough to carry out a literary revolution at the same moment. For if poetry and imaginative literature are to be directly used in the struggle, and there is no very good reason why they should be – the most far-reaching reforms are necessary – reforms which practically amount to a return to classicism and the development of a new plain style, something precise and clear and immediately comprehensible to any literate person. This is probably out of the question by now for poetry. Attempts at writing songs or satires – the only forms in which there is much hope – involve definite 'writing down' from intellectuals (culturally bourgeois) to proletarians. Perhaps it can be done, but it can only be a side-show for poets who have known the poetry of self-expression and sophistication.

   With prose, on the other hand, there is a certain amount of hope. At present the propaganda of the left is conducted in a technical and incomprehensible language: it should be possible for the intellectuals to produce a persuasive prose that would be understood by, and that would affect, anyone able to read. What is needed at the moment is clear thinking and the clearing away of muddles – an intellectual counter-attack by the scientifically-minded on the mistakes and deceits of fascism and reaction. An appeal to emotion and 'dynamic' revolutionary feelings is simply opening the way to intellectual fascism.

JULIAN BELL
(King's College, Cambridge)

   Comrade Bell, in his first paragraph, accuses me of a 'grotesque piece of false over-simplification.' He himself, however, has considerably over-simplified the task of refuting what I wrote by attempting to represent my use of certain adjectives (one of which 'static' I, incidentally, did not use at all) which, in their context, were used accurately, as the whole content of my argument. In order that Comrade Bell's subjective formulation may not succeed in entirely obscuring the issue, I will try and present as coherently as possible the substance of his argument.

1. Literature stands above or outside the class-struggle. The struggle for power between bourgeoisie and proletariat, which has invaded every other field of human activity, has somehow kept clear of the sacred precincts of literary traditions. It is therefore unreal to look for a corresponding division between revolutionary and reactionary writers.
2. There is one single literary tradition, the precious heritage of a cultured, educated, sensitive minority, which includes all writers who, 'whatever their class origins, acquire enough

literary training and practice to be able to write poetry.'

3. It is ridiculous to analyse their art in terms of the class-struggle. They are so busily engaged in analysing what it feels like to be themselves and telling the world about it by means of a 'highly developed literary technique' which they find 'ready to hand' that they can have no concern with objective reality.

4. Since at any given moment everyone has the type of mind produced by a historic development of society, and since a 'revolutionary environment' doesn't last for long, revolutionary poetry is 'definitely contemporary and ephemeral.' To win 'immortality' it is necessary to use the 'highly developed literary technique' of the 'European literary tradition' in arousing 'some of the highly-valued emotions,' which unlike a 'revolutionary environment,' are 'comparatively stable.'

5. Consequently, literature can play no important part in the class-struggle. It is the exclusive affair of a minority who, to use F. R. Leavis's words, 'keep alive the subtlest and most perishable parts of tradition. Upon them depend the implicit standards that order the finer living of an age.' They haven't time to carry out a literary revolution and so it is impossible to expect them to write anything intelligible to anyone who hasn't the leisure to study literature carefully.

6. So that for these cultured gentlemen to start writing clearly would merely mean wasting their time 'writing down to proletarians' when they ought to be getting on with the really serious business of the 'poetry of self-expression and sophistication.' Consequently, if they want to play any part as intellectuals in the revolution they must devote themselves to the production of 'persuasive prose.'

Parasitic versus Revolutionary Art

In order to analyse how precisely this assortment of abstract dogmas is related to what I wrote, I must first re-state the fundamental assumption that was implicit in all I wrote; *that all art is class art.* The works with which I dealt are published and read exclusively by the leisured classes; their authors, whatever their class origins, are to an increasing extent parasitic on 'liberal-minded' publishers or wealthy connoisseurs. By their class-position they are cut off from the life and struggles of the working class. Their parasitic position prevents them from having an objective analysis of society; if they are to write anything of revolutionary content which reaches a wider circle of readers than the intelligentsia, they must break completely with their old way of living *and with their old tradition of writing.* Very few of them are able for various reasons to do this. Those who, like Louis Aragon, succeeded in doing so, become revolutionary writers in a new tradition. But for those who continue to write only what it pays a bourgeois publisher to publish, and which is read only by the bourgeois intelligentsia, the term 'bourgeois artist' is an accurate description. Insofar as they attack the existing order in their work, it is from a purely anarchist (Lawrence, Aldington, Pound) or despairing (Eliot, Joyce, Huxley) point of view, in no way objectively dangerous to the bourgeoisie. If it becomes so, as in Germany to-day, the publishers cease publishing and deprive the artist of his means of life.

It is a completely unhistorical view of literary history to see it as a smooth, all-embracing, traditional process, unrelated to the economic and political forces at work in society. The tremendous forces of energy generated during the period of the bourgeois revolution in which the struggle for power with feudalism was at its most crucial period, found expression in the terrific artistic revolutions of the Elizabethan drama and the Dutch painters. Their work was born out of the revolutionary struggle and victory of the bourgeoisie; is it therefore 'definitely contemporary and ephemeral'?; or does Comrade Bell regard it as a historical accident that a number of people who were good at expressing themselves happened to appear at that particular place and time?

Of course these revolutions made full use of the achievements of feudal art – just as Socialism makes use of the technical achievements of capitalism – but its ideological content and purpose, and its readers are different. Thus, although the literary tradition of a revolutionary class arises out of the tradition of the established order, it is completely unhistorical to identify the two. Although the one emerges from the other, at every decisive historical epoch when the struggle for power is on the order of the day, the two traditions, one in a decaying, one in an embryonic form, exist antagonistically side by side.

What are the characteristics of bourgeois literature in decline? Briefly they are these. The bourgeois writers are acutely conscious that they belong to a declining class, for they are the most sensitive of the bourgeois ideologists; as it were the antennae of bourgeois culture. Owing to their isolation, however, this consciousness is not interpreted objectively as the decline of their class. It seems the decline of 'culture,' of 'civilization.' They cling to what seems the one stable element in a collapsing world, their own literary tradition. From this arises the general concept of a contradiction between art and life, between the life of the artist and the life of society. The world is hastening to complete collapse; the only lasting, eternal factor is the literary tradition. Consequently the only people who matter are the leisured and cultured few who can devote themselves to the study of literature.

Position of Revolutionary Writers

Comrade Bell is quite right that this tradition cannot be used as a revolutionary weapon in the class-struggle. That is exactly why it is not the only tradition. There is to-day everywhere a tremendous spontaneous development of working-class literature, although as yet little is published and most is technically backward. More and more younger writers realising that the logical direction of bourgeois art in decline is towards a kind of artistic sophism, a super-subjectivity, realising that the art of the future is the art of the ruling class of the future, go over to the revolutionary movement as the only possible solution to their own cultural problems. Because of their superior technical education, they form the vanguard of the class-struggle on this front. This is a spontaneous process arising historically out of the position we are in, on the brink of a new round of wars and revolutions, so that Comrade Bell's last point has no significance. The energies released by the revolutionary movement will find expression in a revolutionary art, whether or not our intellectuals devote their time to 'writing down to proletarians.'

In England already several younger poets are groping towards a simple revolutionary technique. If the process is slow, it is because the struggle has not yet assumed such acute forms in England, and the content of the movement, arising out of no direct participation in revolutionary struggles, often takes the subjective form of a purely 'literary' revolution. But the inherent contradiction of this position of a revolutionary literature written for the bourgeois intelligentsia daily hastens the process of differentiation between two literatures, the disintegrating tradition of the bourgeoisie, or the gathering strength of revolutionary art. The true development of European culture lies only with this last. The art of the bourgeoisie disintegrates and reaches a dead end and, at the same time, as the social order of the men who published it, paid for it and read it.

*LEFT?**

Finally, as the class struggle nears its decisive stage, disintegration of the ruling class and the old order of society becomes so active, so acute, that a small part of the ruling class breaks away to make common cause with the revolutionary class, the class which holds the future in its hands. Just as in former days, part of the nobility went over to the bourgeoisie, so now part of the bourgeoisie goes over to the proletariat. Especially does this happen in the case of some of the bourgeois ideologists, who have achieved theoretical understanding of the historical movement as a whole. – *The Communist Manifesto, 1848.*

IN England in the literary field this tendency has expressed itself chiefly in the revolutionary fermentation in the work of the younger poets – W. H. Auden, Charles Madge, Stephen Spender, C. Day Lewis, Richard Goodman, H. V. Kemp. As the crisis deepens, the situation more and more urgently demands a choice between revolution and reaction. The collapse into subjectivity of Eliot, Joyce, or Pound shows more and more clearly the fate of those who refuse to admit the necessity of choice. The traditional artist's 'impartiality' is unmasked as a denial of the class struggle – as a powerful instrument in the hands of the possessing class who would prefer to keep in their hands the means of production without a struggle. And the bankruptcy of the older writers – for the most part comfortably assured of a parasitic position under the present system – becomes clearer and clearer to the younger writers, faced with unemployment, with no prospect of living as writers, and for the first time beginning to consider objectively the causes and the way out of the position with which they and we are faced.

Thus there are the beginnings of a politically-conscious revolutionary literature for the first time in the history of English culture. At the same time there exists side by side with it a very dangerous attempt to deck out the old class literature in new revolutionary-utopian trappings, to exploit the leftward movement among the younger students and intellectuals in order to serve up the old dope in a 'revolutionary' form, to make a literary fashion of 'revolution' among bourgeois intellectuals whilst denying the possibility of the growth of a genuinely revolutionary literature with a new class-basis. The fashionable reactionary critics confuse the two tendencies; it is in their interests to do so. And it is not easy to make a clear demarcation between them. Often they exist side by side in the work of a single writer. But as the crisis matures the division becomes clearer. And the differentiation is essential to the growth of a revolutionary literature. It is essential that this second tendency should be ruthlessly exposed, or otherwise the movement will be poisoned at its source. It is the task of this essay to provide a basis for this demarcation.

The fundamental antagonism of these two tendencies was exposed most clearly in a recent controversy between Stephen Spender and Charles Madge on the question of Poetry and Revolution. The question disputed was the fundamental question of the objective participation of the writer in the class-struggle. Spender's article is so significant as to be worth quoting in detail.

> Of human activities, writing poetry is one of the least revolutionary. The states of being a rentier, a merchant, a capitalist, contribute their bits to revolution, they actively crumble(!) But the writing of a poem in itself solves the poem's problem. If a poem is not complete in itself, if its content spills over into our world of confused emotions, then it is a bad poem.

This is very interesting, because it is in seemingly complete contradiction to the revolutionary-utopian expressions of some of his poetry. It shows quite clearly that Spender adheres to the doctrine that has become fundamental to the bourgeois writers of our epoch – the contradiction between art and life, between the life of the artist and the life of society. The world of the artist is considered as a metaphysical abstraction unrelated to the world in which he lives, which produced him and his art. In so far as he is related to it, it is as the 'impartial' observer.

And there is a fundamental confusion – a confusion between the 'impartiality' of the bourgeois writer and the objectivity of the revolutionary writer. Bourgeois 'impartiality' is a denial of the objective fact of the class struggle, a deliberate self-protection from the conclusion to which an objective study of the world to-day will lead. But there is no middle position between revolution and reaction. Not to take sides is to support the *status quo*, to prefer to leave things as they are rather than risk losing one's own position, and thus to remain indirectly an instrument of reaction. But an objective study of the world as it is to-day, an objective contrast between the capitalist world and the Soviet Union, between the conditions of bourgeoisie and proletariat in this country, can lead to only one conclusion – a revolutionary conclusion, which bourgeois 'impartiality' strives to mask.

And so the objective writer cannot remain a 'detached' observer of society. He must actively participate in the revolutionary struggles of society if he is not going to collapse into the super-subjectivity of the older writers. He must emphatically deny the contradiction between life and art.

In his reply to Stephen Spender, Charles Madge showed himself more or less clearly aware of this. He realises that there is no ideal poets' world unrelated to the reality.

> The problem which the poem solves is not the poem's but the poet's problem. As a consequence of the poem it is the poet, or his reader, who moves. There is no world but the world and that world is the poem's world.

And yet this reply is inadequate. He does nothing to clarify the subjective confusions and contradictions, into which Spender has fallen, by reducing them to an objective terminology. Against Spender's counter-revolutionary dogmas he offsets his own revolutionary dogmas. This is not due to an accidental lack of clarity of exposition. It is due to a contradiction in the work even of the genuinely revolutionary and leftward moving poets.

This is not hard to explain. It is because, although politically they have rejected their class, they are still writing mainly for it. Their training as writers has been a direct barrier to the writing of straightforward revolutionary poetry which can only be overcome by direct participation in revolutionary struggles. C. Day Lewis makes great play of the fact that Lawrence, who came from the working class, is not read by the working class. But this is true precisely because he cut himself off from his class, because he became so isolated from it that he ceased to represent it. In a passage in *The Rainbow* he gives an extraordinarily clear and moving description of class-oppression. But, as he himself was divorced from industry and never participated in a single struggle of his class, he never conceived of it acting as a unit to emancipate itself. Thus, instead of struggling against class oppression and exploitation, he railed against 'industrialism,' and ran half round the world looking for an escape into some more primitive non-industrial form of life. The working-class is not in a position to run round the world looking for an escape from 'industrialism.' That is why it does not read Lawrence. It may seem contradictory to believe that these young intellectual writers can more directly write for the workers than could the miner's son, Lawrence. But who represented the interests of the workers, the ex-railwayman, Jimmy Thomas, or Lenin who was by his class-origin cut off from industry?

This contradiction is as transient a phenomenon as the disintegration of the bourgeoisie. It can no more become the basis of a lasting literary movement than the section of left-moving intellectuals can become a permanent class differentiated from bourgeoisie and proletariat. The lesson of Germany shows perfectly clearly that as the crisis matures, choice between one side or the other is demanded by the conditions of existence. Only a particular and temporary set of historical circumstances can allow this section to appear for a time as an independent class which is not compelled to throw in its full weight with bourgeoisie or proletariat. As the struggle develops, they must follow the process they have started to its logical conclusion – active participation in the class struggle. For within the framework of dying capitalism they can only continue their existence as official apologists for the *status quo* – all other forms of expression, however non-political, are banned as dangerous in the 'totalitarian' state, and the drive towards Fascism in the 'democratic' countries is rapidly imposing similar restrictions on freedom of expression.

And there are hopes that, in spite of the obscurity and crudity which are the growing pains of every vital movement, by certain of these poets a clear and powerful verse is being evolved. There is no ambiguity about this.

> Once masters struck with whips: of recent
> Years by being jolly decent
>   For these are cuter;
> Fostering the heart's self-adulation
> Would dissipate all irritation,
> Making a weakened generation
>   Completely neuter.

Let fever sweat them till they tremble,
Cramp rack their limbs till they resemble
    Cartoons by Goya;
Their daughters sterile be in out,
May cancer rot their herring gut,
The circular madness on them shut
    Or paranoia.

This is a far more virile and direct revolutionary form than Stephen Spender's:

They walk home remembering the straining red flags;
And with pennons of song fluttering through their blood,
They dream of the World State
With its towns like brain centres and its pulsing arteries.

Of such verse Madge correctly observes: 'They get relief from speaking of the horrors they have seen and from pictures fulfilling their wish for a better world.' This poetry is only a kind of Utopian wish-fulfilment. It is not the poetry of revolutionary struggle. It is the poetry of revolution as a literary fashion, not as an historic reality. No wonder Spender is the pet of the bourgeois-liberal critics. If this is the revolution, then there is no need to fear such an idealist romantic affair! But this is not the revolution. This is only the intelligentsia playing at revolution.

And to realise the full difference between these two tendencies, compare Stephen Spender's

The architectural gold-leaved flower
From people ordered like a single mind,
    I build.

with Louis Aragon's

I am a witness to the crushing of a world out of date,
I am a witness drunkenly to the stamping out of the bourgeois.

Was there ever a finer chase than the chase we give
to that vermin which flattens itself in every nook of the cities
I sing the violent domination of the bourgeoisie by the proletariat
for the annihilation of that bourgeoisie.
for the total annihilation of that bourgeoisie.

There can be no doubt that the future is with the revolutionary participator and not the 'impartial' observer, nor the romantic-utopian idealist. And just as out of the rise to power of the bourgeoisie, out of the violent shattering of the feudal remnants, out of the violent expropriation of the independent producers, was born the tremendous revolutionary movement of the Elizabethan drama, so out of the violent struggle for power between bourgeoisie and proletariat, as the Communist Party in this country develops from its sectarian beginnings to a mass revolutionary party, there will arise a revolutionary literature stronger and more various than any which preceded it.

THE STRUGGLE FOR POWER IN WESTERN EUROPE*

I

To understand the mechanics of the class struggle in the capitalist countries, and in particular the highest point of the struggle since 1921 – the fight of the Austrian workers against Fascism – it is necessary first of all to be clear on two points concerning the nature of the crisis and the nature of Fascism.

1. What is the fundamental cause of the present crisis? It is the contradiction between the highly developed productive forces, mass-production with an extensive division of labour, and the property-relation whereby an individual producer appropriates the product of this social labour. That is to say, the working masses can only buy back, under the existing scheme of property-relations, a fraction of what they produce. The surplus has to be exported: and this can only be done with

a continually expanding market. The division of the world market is now almost complete. We are in the period of the general crisis of capitalism, from which no permanent recovery is possible, and from which individual countries can only improve their position at the expense of others by economic warfare (dumping, tariff-war – which further intensify the crisis by narrowing the home market) and ultimately by open war for the re-division of the world market. That war has already begun in the Far East and in South America.

If this analysis is correct, what is the reason for the apparent recovery of 1933, whose symptoms are the slight decline in unemployment and the sharp rise in production? The answer is, that it is exclusively of a military-inflationist character; that is, it is either based on the production of war-materials, or else it is speculative production, based not on any increased market, but simply on a desperate and unfounded hope that sales will increase.

This is borne out by all the statistics available for 1933. Kuusinen, in his report to the Thirteenth Plenum of the Communist International, gives the following statistics:

> In the U.S.A. the output of steel increased by 3,800,000 tons.
>
> In France the output of pig iron and steel rose 24 per cent.
>
> In England the output of pig iron and steel increased 30 per cent; in Japan, 23 per cent.
>
> In Germany the index of production (1924=100) rose from 64.1 to 74 in the course of the year. *But this increase was only in the steel, iron, coal and automobile industries. In all other industries the level was lower even than 1932.*
>
> The shares of Vickers, Schneider-Creusot, Skoda, Krupp, and Bofors all rose in value; the dividends remained stable or increased.

In so far as other countries have 'recovered,' as in the United States cotton industry, the pick-up was purely speculative, and in many cases already the decline has set in. So the conclusion is: since war materials find no ultimate consumer in the market, and since the money to buy them must therefore remain a drag on the other industries which impedes recovery, war-production further degrades the whole structure of economy. We are heading straight for war; it is on war that the 'recovery' mongers are speculating, and on no fundamental chance of improvement within the existing system.

2. Faced with this position, the political problems facing the ruling class are:

(1) To transfer the main weight of the crisis on to the shoulders of the working class.

(2) To exploit to the maximum the divisions in the various class forces whose interests are opposed to it, and to win over the petty bourgeoisie, and as large a stratum of the backward workers and peasants as possible, to the side of big capital against the working-class movement.

(3) To protect itself from revolution in the event of war breaking out.

This is achieved through Fascism. Fascism strives to cripple the working-class movement by murdering and torturing its leaders, suppressing its legal organisations and press, removing the right to strike in defence of wages and conditions, and all political rights whatsoever. Fascism exploits the Nationalist feelings of the petty bourgeoisie to divert their hostility towards the existing regime by whipping up a chauvinist frenzy against some foreign scapegoat – in Germany the Jews; in Poland the Ukrainian minority.

But it is of fundamental importance to be under no illusions as to the class basis of Fascism. It is the dictatorship of big capital, although its terrorist troops may be drawn from the petty bourgeoisie. It is only necessary to show the class-composition of Hitler's 'General Economic Council,' of whom nine are industrialists, four are bankers, and two are big agrarians. It is not accidental that Hitler has not carried out a single detail of the 'Socialist' side of his programme, which included nationalisation of the trusts, the banks, and the big department stores.

This is of great importance, because it shows that there is

nothing revolutionary about Fascism. Although the forms of rule may be different, the class-content is the same. Fascism develops quite logically out of capitalist democracy – it is in no sense a revolutionary break with it. What we are witnessing is a process of fascisation through the democratic machinery. Brüning, von Papen, and Schleicher 'constitutionally' prepared the way for Hindenburg to invite Hitler (also 'constitutionally,' through the single loophole in the 'water-tight' Weimar constitution) to power. At no period was there a revolutionary overthrow of the democracy. And those gentlemen who talk about democracy versus dictatorship are therefore completely distorting the actual historical process.

What is the attitude of the working-class movement to these developments?

Let us take first of all the Second International. The Second International still contains the majority of the Social Democratic parties of Europe. The main basis of its formation was the buying off of certain sections of the better-paid strata of the working class by the granting of social reforms, and winning them to the belief that a peaceful, democratic road to Socialism was possible, because capitalism was able to surmount its crises, and the centralisation of the means of production would one day evolve into Socialism. There is no need to go into a lengthy theoretical disproof of this theory when historical practice has so conclusively demonstrated its falsity. It is necessary only to note that by slurring over the question of the ownership of the means of production it also evades the question of the conquest of power. The insistence on the 'democratic' transition to Socialism against 'dictatorship' and 'bloody revolution' has in practice led to the defence of the 'democratic' bourgeois rule against the revolutionary working class, while all the time the 'democratic' bourgeois is behind their backs preparing for Fascism. In the last resort Social Democracy is driven to take up arms in defence of democracy – against the working class (15,000 were killed when the Social Democrats put down the Spartacus revolt; 60,000 arrests were made by the Labour Government in India). Even after the crisis and the introduction of Fascism, the Social Democrats remain true to themselves to the last. Ten years ago the German Social Democrats told us how Germany was different from a backward country like Italy, and that in 'democratic' Germany the peaceful transition to Socialism is still possible. And now we still hear that England is 'different' from Germany.

In their defence of 'democracy' the Social Democrats have always been compelled to refuse united action with the Communists. True to themselves to the last, the German Social Democrats in 1932 at the Presidential elections instructed their supporters to vote for the 'democrat' Hindenburg against the only workers' candidate, the communist Thaelmann, under the slogan 'Wähl Hindenburg–Schlag Hitler.' And less than a year later Hindenburg 'constitutionally' called Hitler to power!

With the deepening crisis the influence of the Communists increased rapidly. So in order to preserve its independence, and at the same time to preserve the support of the workers, Social Democracy is compelled to face in two directions – to show the bourgeoisie its absolute loyalty and to present to the revolutionary workers revolutionary phrases without giving any lead in the immediate struggles. The new 'revolutionary' programme of what is left of German Social Democracy contains not a single mention of the word strike. And this is typical. D. Z. Manuilsky, at the 17th Congress of the Communist Party of the Soviet Union, describes the process as follows:

We are for Socialism but without the proletarian revolution, the Second International announces.

We are for the proletarian revolution but without the proletarian dictatorship, declares the German Social Democracy. We are solely for the restoration of democracy. We are for the proletarian dictatorship, but ask the Comintern to make an exception of Scandinavia, where democracy is still possible, declares Friedrich Adler.

We are for organisational unity, but against the united front, the Second International announces.

And the former Spanish Minister, Largo Caballero, comments on this thesis in the following manner: There exists no difference between us and the Communists. What is the use of amalgamating if we are already the same?

The Roosevelt programme is our programme, says the Second International.

The Roosevelt programme is the programme of Italian Fascism, replies Mussolini.

Not reforms, but the question of power is on the day, blusters the Second International.

We are prepared to seize power if the President of the Republic calls on us, replies the Socialist Party of France.

In the English Labour Party we see a division of labour between the 'Rights,' Citrine and Henderson and Co., vying with each other in praise for Roosevelt and the League of Nations and abuse of the U.S.S.R., while the 'Lefts,' Cripps and Cole, tell the workers of the wonderful things they will do when they come to power, and if then they are in control of the Labour Party. Objectively both hold back the struggle of the workers against the National Government here and now. Both reject the united front, though the 'Lefts' assure us that they are doing so only because of Party discipline. When the lessons of Germany and Austria cry out for working-class unity here and now, still they hold back the workers from immediate and direct united action by telling them that all they have to do is to wait three years till the next election. True to themselves to the last.

In sharp opposition to the theory and practice of the democratic transition from Capitalism to Socialism stands the Communist International. It has always resolutely put forward the slogan of class against class. It has continually emphasised that the fundamental contradictions of the capitalist system of production will inevitably lead to a crisis from which only the conquest of power by the working class is a way out. In the period of stabilisation from 1924–29, when Tarnow, the leader of the German Social Democratic trade unions, was talking of Ford as more revolutionary than Marx, when the English I.L.P. leaders were saying that American prosperity had proved the Marxian theory of crisis and the law of the absolute impoverishment of the working class to be out of date, only the Communist International foretold the crash and consistently advocated the revolutionary way out. The Communist International repeatedly declared that bourgeois democracy, so long as the means of production and of propaganda – press, wireless, cinema – remain in the hands of the capitalists, can be constitutionally converted overnight into Fascism by means of special powers, emergency laws, etc. Whilst the land and the factories, the police and the armed forces, remain in the hands of the capitalists, the political rights of the workers can be removed at a moment's notice without the least difficulty – unless the working class is prepared to take up a revolutionary stand against the capitalist class.

There is no need to make an elaborate theoretical justification of this policy here. History has proved its correctness.

And it was because of its correct understanding of history that the Communist International was able to develop correct organisational forms to meet the tasks confronting it. Only the Communists could see the necessity of building up a highly organised system of Party nuclei at the key-points of industry and transport, in the streets and in the factories, wherever the workers live and work. Only the Communist Party saw the necessity of doing systematic, illegal work in the armed forces.

But it is nevertheless true that the Communist Parties have lagged behind the development of the crisis. In some countries systematic police terror was able partially to break down their contact with the mass of the workers. In others the exposure of the Social Democrats was not conducted with sufficient clarity, with the result that the Party was isolated from the Social Democratic workers The practice of factory work and work in the trade unions lagged behind the theory. And though 1932–33 saw a rapid growth in the power and influence of the Communist Parties all over Europe, yet where Fascism struck its heaviest blow – in Germany – the Party, having only the advanced section of the workers behind it, was forced to retreat, rather than ensure the destruction of the vanguard of the workers without the masses behind them. It was not destroyed, as the gentlemen who believe in 'peaceful means' would have us think. One has only to read the statements of Hitler, Goering, and Goebbels to realise that it has maintained its organisation and is carrying on the struggle. The circulation of the illegal press of the C.P. is greater than its legal circulation, and even a Berlin chief-of-police is compelled to admit that more than half is printed in Germany. The factory work is better now than ever before. In Germany, and all over Europe, the working class has not been defeated by the Fascist terror. It is moving on to the counter-offensive.

That is the background against which the Austrian rising took place.

II

Just as in a strike, the exact point at which the workers down tools may be some apparently quite trivial incident – a single case of victimisation – and to this single incident is attached the whole accumulated bitterness of years of exploitation, so some incident of seemingly minor importance can give the signal for a revolutionary outbreak which challenges the whole rotten system. The sharp revolutionary struggle in Western Europe began with the Anarchist workers' putsch in Spain. The putsch was probably inspired by reactionary provocation, and might have ended in a little senseless shooting, as previous attempts had done. But on this occasion the Spanish working classes, at the peak point of political activity and enthusiasm after the recent elections, followed the lead of the Anarchists. Although the Communist Party saw clearly that at that moment successful insurrection was impossible, yet to have stood aside when the masses of the workers were moving into action would have forfeited their confidence for years to come. So the Communist Party of Spain threw all its forces into the struggle and converted it from a senseless terroristic putsch into a serious political struggle of the working class. The struggle was defeated. But the working-class movement has not been defeated; and the Communist Party of Spain, both for its correct political analysis before the outbreak and its resolute leadership during the struggle, stands out more clearly than ever before as the real leader of the Spanish workers.

And it was the revolutionary struggle in Spain which set light to the smouldering indignation of the French working class. The Stavisky scandal threw into very sharp relief the whole rottenness and corruptness of the capitalist regime. As the Democrat Deputy Dulot said: 'This time it is perhaps the trial of the ruling classes, opened through the prosecution of the profiteers.'

Fascism made a tremendous effort to exploit the mass movement for its own purposes. For the first time something like a Fascist mass youth movement was launched. But they were not altogether successful in capturing the leadership. After the first Royalist demonstrations had been fired on, the working class took the affairs into its own hands, under the leadership of the Communist Party and of the Red Trade Unions. For five hours on 9th February a fierce fight took place for the possession of the streets. Hundreds were wounded, and several killed by revolver bullets. A united general protest strike was called for the Monday, and it met with a practically unanimous response. On the 16th a mass demonstration under the leadership of the Communist Party to the funeral of six of the killed workers was attended by 200,000 workers. And though now the working-class movement has temporarily subsided, it has at no point been defeated. At any moment it may flare up again.

The barricade fighting in the streets of Paris was, as it were, the link in the chain of the revolutionary upsurge that connects the Austrian with the Spanish rising. In Austria, for years the Social Democratic Party had been in a practically unchallenged position. Every fourth worker was a member. They had won complete control after the war – and exercised it in the interests of the capitalists. Although an extensive system of social services and public works had been built up, the land and the factories remained the property of the capitalist class. After the war Social Democracy stood in between the workers and a decisive blow against capitalism. When the first revolutionary wave of 1919–21 had subsided, the capitalists bit by bit regained their footing in the State. In March 1933, after Dollfuss had captured power by a very narrow majority at a previous election, although the Social Democrats still had behind them the mass of the workers, and still had important key points in the local administration, Dollfuss was able silently to dispose of Parliament. The bourgeois Liberal *New Statesman* describes the policy of the Social Democrats in the months that followed like this:

> What is the Socialist Party's record during the long months of violation of the Republican Constitution, of incessant provocation to the workers and challenges to their leaders since last March? Dr. Otto Bauer, the political genius of the Party, has given in interviews a list of concrete efforts made by the Socialists to come to an agreement with Dr. Dollfuss which would have enabled a united democratic front to be formed to combat the Nazi terror. He declares that every attempt – even that of a conditional offer to give Dollfuss the power to govern for two years without Parliament, was shattered on the determination of Dollfuss … to establish autocratic rule in Austria and destroy the democratic Republic.

It is the same old story. In the interests of preserving bourgeois democracy against dictatorship, the revolutionary struggle to overthrow the system is sabotaged, the united front with the Communist Party is rejected while an offer of a united front is made to the bourgeoisie, who then quite calmly introduce Fascism over the heads of a divided and paralysed working-class movement. As the *New Statesman* goes on to say: 'Surely no reactionaries ever had a harder task in provoking conflict with the Left than Dollfuss and Fey.' The Social Democrats meekly allowed themselves to be kicked out of one position after another, until all chance of a successful struggle was gone.

But meanwhile the influence of their Party was necessarily declining among the workers. More and more the small and weak Austrian Communist Party was building up a united front, not with Dollfuss against Hitlerism, but of the working class against capitalism. The strike wave was rising.

On 30th January, the Heimwehr occupied the capital of the Tyrol, Innsbruck, on a pretext of 'defensive action' against the Nazis. On 7th February, the Upper Austrian Heimwehr followed suit. They marched into Linz and Steyr (strongholds of Social Democratic administration) and demanded the installation of Government Commissioners.

On 10th February, Dollfuss demanded the 'reorganisation' of the State. The Social Democratic premises in Vienna were smashed up, and the workers' clubs in Innsbruck. At this point the Communist Party, in its illegal paper, launched the slogan: 'Crush Fascism before it crushes you! Down tools at once, strike, elect committees of action to lead the struggle in every factory! Disarm the Fascists! The weapons into the hands of the workers! General strike! Away with the Government of hangmen!' The edition was enthusiastically received. But the Communist Party was too small to launch the struggle by itself.

On 10th February, Herr Seitz, the Social Democrat Mayor of Vienna, was deprived of all control of the police force. In spite of the fact that they had repeatedly declared they would defend the constitutional rights of Vienna, the Social Democratic Party for two critical days sat still and did nothing. But on 12th February, when the police began searching for arms in the workers' quarters in Linz, the working class took matters into its own hands and fought back fiercely. All over Austria the struggle broke out whilst the leadership of the Social Democratic Party was still discussing what legal avenues were left open to it.

Without a well-tried revolutionary leadership, without a carefully organised plan of insurrection, after two fatal days had been allowed to slip by whilst the Fascists consolidated their position, the insurrection was doomed to defeat before it started. But it was an example of the astonishing power of the workers' movement that it was able to throw up its own leadership, and work out its own plan of action. For nearly a week a desperate struggle was carried on, during which the Fascists were forced to bring out artillery against their own working class. The whole of the working class was flung into action, or else the revolution could not possibly have lasted for that length of time. In spite of their inferiority of armament, in spite of the lack of leadership, yet the working class, once it had taken the road of revolutionary struggle, followed without hesitation and carried on the struggle until all their arms were exhausted. And meanwhile Dollfuss, with tears trickling down his cheeks, as he declared that it was the saddest week in his life, busily set to work hanging the wounded prisoners.

III

What are the main lessons of the Austrian rising? First of all, it explodes completely all the reactionary ideas that have been brought forward that it is impossible for the working class to capture power by revolutionary means. Kuusinen writes in his speech to the Thirteenth Plenum:

> This experience has shown that the opportunities for police and troops to use many types of arms in towns where insurgents can hide in houses and utilise the tactical advantages of this or that block of houses is very restricted. In these conditions the insurgents are able to utilise various types of passive and active weapons against the military-technical resources of the Government. It is sufficient to recall the Hamburg rebellion, or the street-fighting in Chapei, where barricades and hastily dug trenches served as serious obstacles to the movements of armoured cars. Hand-to-hand fighting in towns, the fighting for every single house and every single corner calls for tremendous moral firmness on the part of the troops, and serious fighting threatens to demoralise them.

The Austrian rising is yet another practical demonstration of the power of the working class to conquer by direct revolutionary tactics.

They were defeated, but they were not defeated because they took up arms. They were defeated because they were not under the leadership of a revolutionary party. What concretely did this mean? It meant in the first place that no plan of organised insurrection had been worked out beforehand, and there was no experienced leadership. The movement had to throw up its own leaders. It meant that the struggle began in an unorganised way after the correct moment had gone by. It meant that there had been no systematic illegal work in the armed forces to bring them over to the revolution. It meant that there were no experienced nuclei of revolutionary forces inside the factories to lead and guide the struggle before and after the insurrection.

But the temporary defeat of the Austrian workers is not a defeat for the international working class. Only in one small sector, where the revolutionary movement was backward and isolated, has the working class been beaten back, and that only after a tremendous struggle. The absolute necessity of revolutionary leadership for a successful armed struggle is made clearer than ever before to the European working class. And as the decisive struggles rapidly approach, so by the example of the Austrian movement will the working class gather strength in its own power to overthrow capitalism by direct struggle, and throw aside the gentlemen who prefer the 'democratic' road to Fascism to the revolutionary road to Soviet power.

NOTES ON THE TEACHING OF HISTORY AT CAMBRIDGE*

CAMBRIDGE History is not even a coherent account of the history of the British bourgeois state and its clashes with other states; it illustrates the confusions and inconsistencies of thought which are a necessary element of capitalist society because the capitalist class cannot even be said to know itself:

the true history of capitalist society can only be written by the proletariat.

Cambridge History is class history, but it is confused class history; it is only with the development of Fascism that the exigencies of controlled propaganda in defence of the bourgeoisie during its last struggle to retain power force a coherent and conscious exposition of its ideology as such. Therefore we must look for the beginnings of Fascist history in Cambridge, but we must not forget that the old less militant 'liberal' history is more insidious and perhaps more successful as dope. The British capitalist class may therefore be expected to cling to it more tenaciously, especially as Britain is now one of the 'backward' countries.

In examining the course of study for the Historical Tripos, the first thing we notice is a confusion of aims. This is brought out by studying the relation of historical to other studies, and the division of the field of history into 'subjects' and 'periods' for purposes of lectures and examinations. This confusion has its advantages because it allows for individual adherence to true (Marxist) history on the part of teachers and students at present, but we may be permitted to ask how long this freedom will be allowed even to those who for examination purposes, in order to prevent the possibility of victimisation, take an opportunist line and slightly 'bourgeoisify' that Marxism.

The confused aims of Cambridge History are of course due to general contradictions in capitalist society outside the academic field, but here we must notice especially two important facts: the lack of an accepted philosophy of history; and the consequent ignorance of what constitutes historical evidence and historical fact.

The prevailing philosophy of history is of course idealism, history being regarded as 'really' the unfolding of 'ideas'; but there are remnants of crude bourgeois materialism, utilitarianism, 'economic interpretation,' and so on. It is noticeable that the Hegelian idealism of the Historical Faculty has no relation at all to the Realism which prevails in the Moral Sciences Faculty, while most of the lecturers on history are content with a vague ethical idealism which derives from a muddled popular current of thought rather than from technical philosophy. The usual attitude of academic historians to the question of what is an historical fact is a simple belief in the possibility of giving an impartial account of what happened in the past, and an emphasis on the study of documents. But what actually happens is that the documents are always documents in the history of thought, and that the facts, except in early history, are rarely reported in any detail. The scientific notion of a significant generalisation is not understood at all, but generalisations are made which are consistent with bourgeois ideology as a whole, while being regarded as contributions to absolute truth. It has already been remarked that History in Cambridge is not related to Philosophy; its relation to the history of thought is a curious one, because it is often a substitute for it, but it never makes clear, except in criticising Catholic ideology in medieval history (and this is consistent with the revolutionary role of the bourgeoisie three hundred years ago), the relations between thought and action. The relation of History to Politics is not made clear; political theory is regarded often as an abstract study in association, as if there were a permanent problem of how to live in a community, running through all time, independently of particular historical circumstances. Contemporary politics are rarely related to the past, the curious but significant superstition existing that the story of the immediate past cannot be history at all. The relation of History to Literature is usually no more than a few short references to great writers who flourished, and no attempt is made to link up styles of art and architecture with the ideology of the time. Social History is regarded as a limited study of domestic living, looked at apparently for the fun of the thing, while such matters as industrial technique and the real facts of living in the past are not considered as material for history at all. The law and the constitution are typical fetishes of bourgeois history, and are treated abstractly with little relation to what actually happened, and finally economic history is set off as a mere minor and independent study. The whole sphere of wars and international relations is over-emphasised and treated in isolation.

A final point: Cambridge History is not merely class history, it is mainly national class history. This is a characteristic of capitalist provincialism and insularity, and it is only slightly broken down by the inclusion of imperial history, always political and constitutional in emphasis. And then of course there is no need to emphasise the point that this history is narrowly academic, and unrelated not only to other branches of study, but also to the field of practical activity. In turning to the actual details of the Tripos, we must first of all criticise the lecture, set-book, and examination system. All three have the same effect; they are the weapons used to confine the student's attention to the aspects which the authorities wish to stress, and they usually prevent wider reading, and merely narrow and circumscribe the view of students who take them seriously.

The subjects of the Tripos come under the following four headings: General History, Constitutional History, Economic History, and Political Theory. Special periods are usually taken from one of these headings, and often have a bias towards personalities.

PART I

English Constitutional. – Here the earlier history has the merit of presenting a class analysis, although with no conception of the class struggle. The economic background to legal forms is shown in, for instance, Maitland's medieval work. It would seem that the bourgeoisie is capable of writing the history of the feudal social order which it displaced, because it can free itself from the Catholic religious ideology, and because apart from that the chief documents are factual and not examples of bourgeois aspirations.

But this only applies to the best work, and in Stubbs the illusions of capitalist democracy are read back into the past as far as Magna Carta. The treatment of the English bourgeois revolution is inadequate because it is represented as a stage in the achievement of some generalised 'liberty' which does not exist, and which is in fact the freedom of the capitalist class to set up its political state machine.

So far as more modern times are concerned, there is no explanation of the difference between capitalist aspirations and the actual unwilled eventualities, the forms of the law and the constitution and petty legal arguments being used to try and show that there is a homogenous organised community represented by the capitalist state machine. The facts of 'British government' are not considered at all.

English Economic. – Here the chief characteristics are that strings of facts on industrial and agricultural history, often controversial, are learnt, with no co-ordinating synthesis other than the usual pathetic faith in progress in spite of all evils. The theoretical side of economics is not related to the facts of the past, because, of course, bourgeois economic theories are so confused that they cannot be made to show coherently how the capitalist system developed. There is also a tendency to concentrate on statutes applying to economics and local government, without attempting to show how often they were not applied at all. The true story of primary accumulation can for obvious reasons not be told by these historians, unless when they are dealing with foreign capitalist history.

Political Thought. – This subject is a vague study, and the mere choice of set books from Greek, medieval and capitalist times, as if they all had the same problems and as if their theories were all part of a great continuous effort to find out the truth about political organisation, is enough to condemn it.

PART II

General European. – In this subject no unifying summary is made, the underlying conceptions being personality and national greatness. Attempts are made to give a view of economic factors, but with no correct estimate of their importance. The material on European economic history existing in English is very inadequate. This subject should merge into world history, but it is noticeable that an extra-European view is taken only after the beginnings of imperialist exploitation, and without this reason being given. The general emphasis is on wars, monarchs, empty diplomatic abstractions, while there is little real explanation of the character of the reformed (bourgeois) religion.

Theory of the Modern State. – Here there is no analysis of the meaning of the capitalist state, but only barren metaphysical abstractions. It is true that *The Communist Manifesto* is now among the set books, and that the examiners will accept a disguised Marxism, but the orthodox view that is assumed is a simplified Hegelianism based on the work of the sentimental philanthropist, Bosanquet. Here at least the Cambridge historians give a coherent account of their views. They often temper their Tory idealism with the traditional liberal idealism, and will have nothing to do with the radical materialism of early bourgeois writers, such as the utilitarians. This subject has a legal section, too, for it is easy to talk about law as if it were a fact, and to dispute about rights and obligations on the plane of legal as well as of metaphysical abstraction. Several points are especially important: in the first place, it is assumed that the state is (or represents) the community, and if the community is analysed at all it is analysed structurally by institutions, and not functionally, i.e. according to the relations of production. The ethical approach is fundamental, it being asserted that the end of the state's existence is to promote the 'good' life. It is not explained how the end as an aspiration differs from the end as actually achieved, and no account is given of the difference between the activity of the conscious will and the actual determination of events by social forces. Hegel, of course, does attempt to explain this by an idealist *tour-de-force* that he borrowed from Rousseau, but the English idealists have no better theory than the conversational distinction between higher and lower natures. In a word, even considered from the point of view of capitalist philosophy at its most developed, the theory of the state given us by the Cambridge historians is inadequate, and when faced with the materialist revolutionary dialectic, it is helpless. Some of the historians realise this, and are driven to the view that it is useless to have a philosophical attitude to history at all, and we find the beginnings of a kind of agnosticism, or scepticism, very often among the very men who have come across the philosophy of the revolution, but are afraid to accept it, more through fear of losing their positions than from intellectual timidity, perhaps.

WHAT COMMUNISM STANDS FOR*

I. Primitive and Contemporary Communism Contrasted

To begin with, a distinction must be made between Communism in the sense that the word is used by the Communist Parties now, and between primitive communism, the communism of an order of society which has not yet developed to the stage of the private ownership of the means of production. Whereas primitive communism is essentially based on a low level of productive forces, on a very simple form of pastoral or agricultural production, Communism in the modern sense is based on the collective ownership of large-scale means of production. There is no ethical 'idea' of Communism in the abstract that applies to both forms. The same word covers two distinct types of social organisation. It is to the latter form that I propose to confine myself.

This distinction is simple and elementary. Nevertheless, it is necessary to make it; because hundreds of the more ignorant opponents of Communism have not even found out this elementary fact. In the same way a sharp distinction must be made between Communism in the Marxist sense and between the various communist experiments of earlier periods – early Christian communism, the Taborites, the Social Levellers of the seventeenth century. These were certainly closer to Marxist Communism than was primitive communism, because they arose as a revolt against class exploitation. But they are still sharply distinguished by the fact that they are based essentially on small-scale individual production which puts its products into a common pool, whereas Communism now is based on the collective ownership of socialised industry.

II. Why Capitalism Declines

It is clear, therefore, that the precondition for the rise of Communism is the development of industrial capitalism. The essential features of capitalism are threefold:

(1) The monopoly of the means of production is concentrated in the hands of a small ruling class of industrialists, financiers, and landlords.

(2) Goods are produced not for consumption by the individual producer, but as commodities for sale on a market.

(3) The driving force of society, the motive for production, is not the satisfaction of the needs of society, but the hunt for profits of the capitalist class itself. Production is not for use, but for profit. Every crisis reveals that as soon as production becomes unprofitable, however great may be the needs of society, it is at once discontinued.

To make such a system of production possible, there are two necessary preconditions; at one pole the accumulation of a vast capital in relatively few hands, at the other pole the formation of a propertyless class that has nothing but its labour-power to sell, so that it is forced to continually hire out its labour-power to maintain its existence, and to hire it out in such conditions that the capitalist class invariably has the whip hand in the bargaining.

Both classes can be found in an embryonic form in the medieval city – within the guilds the formation at opposite poles of a patriciate of merchant-monopolists and a semi-proletariat of propertyless journeymen; although for their most rapid development it was necessary for capitalist property relations to smash through the narrow guild restrictions. The principal sources of capital accumulation were the profits of merchant capital, the slave trade, etc. The proletariat was recruited in the main from the countryside. The development of a commodity economy, the development of a market, smashing through the limits of the old feudal self-sufficing economy, giving birth to capitalist relations in the countryside, the simultaneous break up of the bands of feudal retainers, 'set free' a new class. They freed it in a double sense. They freed it from the old feudal services. And, by dispossessing it, they freed it from any personal property in the means of production that it once possessed.

The profit of capital comes from the unpaid labour of the workers, from the new values produced by the workers over and above that necessary for the renewal of the means of production and their own maintenance, and appropriated by the capitalists in virtue of their ownership of the means of production. Consequently, for capital to attain its full profitability, it must find some way of disposing of the surplus of goods that remains over after the payment of wages and maintenance costs. It finds this in three ways. First of all, in its own luxury consumption; but, however much it spends on itself, this can only constitute a small fraction of the total surplus. Secondly, and more important, a big proportion of the surplus is reinvested in an extension of production. What is then left over – often the most important section of all – is disposed of in foreign markets.

Consequently, capitalism must always expand at an increasingly rapid rate. This necessity for continual expansion forcibly extends capitalist property relations all over the world with fantastic speed. The old feudal self-sufficing economy, and the more or less stable Asiatic system of production, are swept away by the flood of cheap commodities. In the political sphere, the feudal land-owners and the absolute monarchy (which represented a temporary balance of power between decaying feudalism and the rising bourgeoisie) are violently swept from power, as in the revolution of 1789–93, or, as in England, forced to an unfavourable compromise.

III. The Period of Permanent Crisis and War

But even in the periods of its most rapid expansion capitalism carried with it the seeds of its own decay. Its historic function was to develop at an unprecedented rate the means of production and technical advance in general, and, whilst it was still engaged in spreading this development all over the world, for all its barbarity, it was the historically appropriate form of social organisation. Capitalism is the system of production appropriate to the period of uncontrolled aggressive outward expansion. But at a very early period it shows itself incapable of organising the productive forces which it has itself brought into being.

Capitalism is only capable of systematic organised production within the limits of a single concern. The scramble for profits between rival producers, and even between different branches of production, makes the organisation of production as a whole an impossibility. The competition between the capitalists forces each of them to continually reinvest his surplus in an extension and improvement of the means of production, which, as the sums spent on more complicated and expensive machinery increase, is accompanied by a continual *relative* diminution of exploitable labour-power. And, since profit can arise only from the direct exploitation of living labour-power, there is a continual tendency for the rate of profit to fall to a limit which makes production no longer profitable. An immense and ever-increasing flow of goods is poured into a market which is *relatively* contracting, owing to the continued relative impoverishment of the mass of the people. There follows a crisis of overproduction.

E. Varga describes the mechanics of such a crisis in these terms:

> To put it more simply: prosperity continues so long as the process of real accumulation is in full swing, as long as new factories, harbours and railways are built, and old machines are replaced by new ones. But as soon as this process reaches a certain conclusion after a considerable number of new production plants have been completed, the demand for the commodities of Division I (means of production) diminishes, entailing a drop in the demand for consumers goods as well, since the workers in Division I are becoming unemployed. At the same time, the supply of commodities increases, since the new and reconstructed factories begin to pour goods into the market. Overproduction already exists, but the open outbreak of the crisis is delayed since the capitalists (who never believe that a prosperity phase will come to an end) are producing for inventory. But production exceeds

consumption to an ever greater extent, until the crisis bursts into the open. (*The Great Crisis and Its Political Consequences*, Martin Lawrence, 1935)

At the time at which Marx wrote, the crises of capitalism were still crises of a period of expansion, which, in spite of their temporarily devastating effects, could still be overcome within the framework of the system by means of the expansion to new markets and the more extensive exploitation of old. But within capitalism there were forces at work, noticeable in an embryonic form even at the time when Marx wrote, whose development has meant that this solution is no longer open to capitalism. The fierce competition between rival capitalists has led continually to the growing concentration of capital, the squeezing out or incorporation of the smaller and less efficient concerns, the division of the markets amongst an ever-diminishing number of industrialists and financiers. This process towards monopoly is inextricably linked to the development of the colonies as closed markets, as a closed source of cheap raw materials, as a closed sphere for the export of capital. It was for this reason that Lenin described this stage in the development of capitalism as the imperialist epoch.

The consequences of this development are two-fold. It is no longer possible for capitalism to overcome its internal crises by outward expansion, since the whole of the world has already been divided up by four or five major powers into colonies, markets, and 'spheres of influence.' Consequently, the nature of the conflicts that are carried on is changed. From 1871 to 1914, the period of imperialist expansion, there was a continual series of wars of expansion, wars of colonisation of the big imperialist powers against small and backward nations; 1914 saw the end of that process. With the development of German capitalism and its famous struggle for a 'place in the sun,' the world was no longer big enough to serve as a market for the rival imperialisms. The epoch of imperialist wars, of wars between the great powers for a redivision of the world, is introduced. Capitalism can no longer solve its problems peacefully; each successive crisis in the imperialist epoch is a prelude to a more desperate world war.

Of course there have been, and, for all I know, there still may be, theories that the growth of monopoly capital, the concentration of capital in fewer and fewer hands, will lead to a planned capitalism, a peaceful division of the world market between a handful of trusts, which will eliminate the need for war. This is not so. The concentration of power in the hands of a few big trusts simplifies the basic antagonisms; it does not eliminate them. The fate of the International Steel Cartel is the fate of all attempts at international capitalist organisation. But there is no need to prove this point theoretically. History has already proved it.

IV. The Limitation of Production under Capitalism

It is not simply because it is unjust that Communists work for the overthrow of capitalism. They do not judge anything by abstract ethical standards. During the period of its rise to power, capitalism was as barbarous as it is today. The early history of the Industrial Revolution, of the old colonial system, of the slave trade, is proof of this. Nevertheless, for all its brutality, it was historically a progressive force. But to-day that is no longer true. Capitalism cannot organise the productive forces that it has called into being. On the contrary, the capitalist property relations have become a check on the development of production. Once the stimulus of a higher rate of profit drove capitalism to expand its production at a colossal rate; now factories are idle, and the market is glutted with unsalable goods, not because there is no consumer for these goods, but because they cannot be sold at a profit. Even in its boom period, capitalism is immensely wasteful of the productive forces of society. Stuart Chase estimated that in America in 1925, in the clothing trade and in the shoe industry, 30 per cent of the working year was lost; that productive waste was 50 per cent in textiles, 81 per cent in the metal industry; that the ratio of workers engaged in production to workers engaged in distribution had fallen from 80:20 in 1850 to 50:50 in 1920 – in other words, that, owing to the cost of marketing, competitive advertising, etc., it cost as much to sell articles as to produce them. And British capitalism, quite apart from incidental waste, is burdened with an immense weight of obsolete exactions, which no force in capitalism has the power to shake off, but which utterly cripple the economic life of the country, and condemn it to a chronic crisis, with a chronic surplus of unemployable labour.

Even in its boom periods, capitalism cannot organise production. And the consequences in the period of crisis are therefore hardly imaginable. According to the economist E. Schultz, the economic loss caused by the world war works out at somewhere around 744 and 833 milliard gold marks, whilst the loss caused by the crisis in U.S.A. and Germany alone between 1929 and 1932 came to 500 milliard gold marks. Capitalism cannot organise production. And the consequence is not only a wanton destruction of productive forces. It is a destruction of human lives. The deaths from starvation, from premature exhaustion, from preventible accidents, from preventible disease, yearly mount up to a more colossal total. And the process reaches its logical culmination in the limitless destruction of imperialist war.

As R. P. Dutt writes:

The most obvious and glaring expression of this process, the burning of foodstuffs, the dismantling of machinery that is still in good condition, strike the imagination of all. But all do not yet see the full significance of these symptoms; first, the expression through these symptoms of the extreme stage of decay of the whole capitalist order; second, the inseparable connection of this process of decay with the social and political phenomena of decay which find their expression in Fascism; and third, the necessary completion and working out of this process in war. For war is only the most complete and most systematic working out of the process of destruction. Today, they are burning wheat and grain, the means of human life. Tomorrow they will be burning living human bodies. *(Fascism and Social Revolution*, Martin Lawrence, 1934)

The continuance of capitalist property relations not only stops any further advance of the productive forces, it endangers life itself. Society must be reorganised, or humanity wiped out. There is only one force capable of this reorganisation – the working class.

V. The Historic Mission of the Working Class
In 1847 Marx and Engels wrote: 'But the bourgeoisie has not only forged the weapons that will slay it; it has also engendered the men who will use these weapons – the modern workers, the PROLETARIANS' *(Manifesto of the Communist Party)*.

As capitalism develops, so it develops the working class. From the very beginning of the formation of the capitalist class there have been revolts of the oppressed semi-proletarian classes, starting with the weavers and metal-workers of thirteenth- and fourteenth-century Flanders. These risings were always defeated. And in many instances these risings put forward demands that were basically reactionary – demands for the return to the sheltered conditions of feudalism and guild production. Thus in the early period in England some of the first working-class organisations had as their specific object the enforcement of sixteenth-century legislation against the introduction of machinery. In the conditions of scattered small-scale production, when the proletariat has not yet been properly constituted as a class, when the most exploited of journeymen has some sort of a chance, albeit a diminishing chance, of becoming a master himself, then, in spite of the intolerable conditions under which he is forced to work, there is no sort of hope of working-class victory, nor even of stable working-class organisation.

But with the concentration of capital the workers also are drawn together. They learn very quickly that organisation is the only weapon of the propertyless class. The conditions of industrial capitalism teach that no advance can be gained without a bitter struggle. And because of the decisive part they play in the productive process; because the very conditions of their life teach them the necessity of organisation and solidarity; because their lack of property means that they have nothing to lose, and consequently they can dare to advance where the middle classes shrink back – for all these reasons the working class is the only class that has the power to overthrow capitalism.

Throughout the whole of history there have been peasant revolts against feudalism and against capitalism. They have always been beaten. And the reason for this is, that although in periods of extreme oppression they may be forced into a defensive alliance, yet peasants remain property owners, often with conflicting interests on the market, their experience teaching them how to compete with one another and not how to organise together; and, consequently, the only fairly stable revolutionary organisations that have been formed in the countryside have been amongst the very poor peasants and the landless labourers. It is not through any ethical subjective superiority, but simply through the daily repeated experience of their living conditions, that the working class is the only consistently revolutionary force in modern society. For the middle classes, the professional classes, the trading classes, the peasants, the students, though they may suffer as badly as the workers during the crisis, are yet not brought face to face with their main enemy – capital. They see the crisis in the form of rising food prices and rising rents, of debts they cannot meet, of competition with the chain stores, and not in the form of speed-up, wage cuts, and dismissals. That is why they are so much more easily swayed to Fascism, to Douglas Credit, to religion, to hysteria, to anything that promises an easy way out without facing realities. And in periods of prosperity they do not get along so badly, they altogether cease to be anti-capitalist. Whereas the working class in the period of the crisis is attacked in the factories and at the Labour Exchanges, and comes directly face to face with its main enemies – the capitalist class and its State machine. And even in periods of 'prosperity' the working class relatively loses ground. Prewar England and pre-crisis U.S.A. were often quoted as examples disproving the Marxist theory of class struggle, and proving the identity of interests of workers and capitalists. But here are the figures. In England between 1893 and 1909 the wealth of the capitalist and landlord classes increased by £336 millions (Inland Revenue statistics), whereas the income of the working class increased by – at a maximum estimate – £30 millions (the Department of Labour, whose statistics covered more than 50 per cent of the working class, estimated £14½ millions); and in America between 1900 and 1924, while the real wealth of the nation increased by 96 per cent, wages increased by – at a maximum estimate – 25 per cent (the British Mission estimates 14 per cent). Thus in the two classic periods of class collaboration the share of the working class in the national income actually declined. Always, and at all times, the interests of the vast majority of the working class are opposed to capitalism. That is what makes the working class the only class capable of the reorganisation of society, and that is why Communism, if it is to accomplish anything, must be rooted in the working-class movement.

VI. The Rise of Scientific Socialism

But it was a long time before the working class was able to give a scientific formulation of its aims in the struggle against capital. In the early history of the working-class movement there are to be found three main tendencies.

First, there is the anarchic revolt that cannot distinguish between the progressive role of the rising heavy industry and the reactionary exploitation of capitalism, and finds its expression in machine wrecking, the fight to re-enact legislation against machinery, etc.

Second, there is the Utopian Socialism, which, though it is founded on ideas of absolute truth, reason, and justice, nevertheless recognises the necessity of a Socialism that will be based on some form of social ownership of large-scale means of production.

Third, there is the revolutionary democracy, which, without having a clear or developed social programme, yet recognises the conquest of State power by the working class as a precondition of any possible transformation of society.

The first of these finds its classic expression in the Luddite movement, the second in Owenism, the third in Chartism, and, more particularly, in the writings of Bronterre O'Brien.

On the basis of these gropings towards Socialism, and on the basis of similar tendencies in European politics, arose scientific Socialism-Marxism – which was able to select what was true and revolutionary from these half-formed theories and reject what was false and irrelevant. These are the essential characteristics of revolutionary Socialism.

(1) Socialism is not seen as an abstract ethical system, but as the culmination of a period of historical development. It is based not on what seems to Marx to be just or true or reasonable in an absolute sense, but on a prolonged and scientific study of the laws of movement of capitalist society.

(2) Socialism is seen as the collective ownership and administration by the working class of large-scale industrial means of production.

(3) The view that capitalism can grow into Socialism is explicitly rejected. The means of production must be wrested by the working class from the hands of the capitalist class.

(4) Socialism that faces reality must base itself on the capture of State power, on the destruction of the old State machine, and its replacement by a new State of a higher type.

(5) The class struggle is not completed by the victory of the working class. For a certain period the repressive machinery of the State must be kept in existence to put down the remnants of the old exploiting classes. That is what is meant by the dictatorship of the proletariat. Only after this resistance has been utterly crushed will the State be enabled to disappear, to 'wither away.'

(6) It will not be possible immediately after the revolution to operate the full Communist programme 'from each according to his abilities, to each according to his need.' For a long time after power has been taken it will be necessary to continue paying wages, etc., not according to need, but according to the amount and quality of work done, according

to formal bourgeois ideas of justice. Only when all scarcity problems have been solved, will it be possible to go over to the complete classless society. Until then, equality means simply the abolition of class exploitation.

VII. The Character of a Reorganised Society

An analysis of the growth and development of capitalism, of the chief results of capitalism in the economic, political, and cultural spheres, of the main forms of exploitation to which the workers are at present subjected, indicates clearly enough the main lines along which society must be reorganised if it is to survive. The salient characteristics of this reorganisation are:

(1) The abolition of classes. It can no longer be tolerated that the whole motive of production should be the profit of a handful of capitalists, so that the world is subject to continual useless waste and periodic devastating crises when production becomes unprofitable for this handful. The first task is the abolition of this monopoly of the means of production, the collective ownership and control by society as a whole of the means of production.

(2) Planned production. The waste, the anarchy, the disorganisation of capitalist competition and capitalist crisis must be brought to an end. At the present level of development of the productive forces, it is absolutely impossible to continue further without the systematic planning of production in the interests of society as a whole.

(3) The mainspring of production must be the satisfaction of the needs of society as a whole, not the profit of a few individuals. To end the present chaos and misery of a society with vastly developed productive forces in which the great majority of the people are still somewhere around, or even far below, the subsistence level, it is necessary to introduce a form of society in which the property relations are no restriction on the extension of production, in which the productive classes are guaranteed the full product of their labour (of course, minus a fund for the replacement and extension of production, for social services, etc.).

(4) It is necessary to put an end to the virtual educational and cultural monopoly of the capitalist classes, by which higher education is restricted within very narrow class limits. It is possible and necessary to extend educational and cultural facilities to a vastly greater extent than the economic and political needs of capitalism make possible.

(5) It is necessary to put an end to the intolerable position in which the whole world is exploited by five or six 'advanced' imperialist powers. It is necessary and possible immediately to liberate the colonial peoples. It is not any defect in the structure of the economy of Europe and America that makes colonial exploitation a necessity. Once again it is simply the needs of a ruling minority.

(6) It is necessary finally to end the inequality of the sexes expressed in difference of social position, difference of wage rates, etc., which exists in capitalist society. This inequality is simply a survival of an obsolete epoch. It is perfectly possible to put an end to it. In fact the conditions of modern society demand that it should be ended. But it will never be ended under capitalism.

These are a few of the characteristics of the necessary reorganisation of society. These are the essential features of Communist society. There is no inherent stupidity of human nature which makes these sensible and necessary measures impossible. The only obstacles are the capitalist property relations, which the capitalist class will fight tooth and nail to defend. For there is one class which stands to lose from the revolution in society which will benefit humanity as a whole.

VIII. The Capitalist State and the Dictatorship of the Proletariat
If proof of what Communism can do is wanted, it is not necessary to look further than the U.S.S.R. The construction of Socialism in Russia started in a country whose economy had been utterly shattered by the world war and the civil wars and wars of intervention that followed. The 1920 index of production was 18 per cent of the 1913 figure. Starting from complete ruin, Russia has been converted from a backward country, dependent

on Anglo-French loan capital, into a powerful independent industrial State. Industrial production has increased fourfold as compared with the 1913 figure. In spite of immense difficulties, Socialist reorganisation of agriculture has produced a far higher yield than was ever possible before. Unemployment has been wiped out. Wage rates have been increased three and four times. A cultural revolution has been carried out. From a country that was predominantly illiterate, Russia has been transformed into a country where the most advanced literary and scientific works, which are lucky very often to sell a few hundred copies in those capitalist countries where they are allowed to be sold at all, are sold in hundreds of thousands. All the reactionary medievalist tendencies of Italy and Germany find their polar opposite, not in the decaying 'democracies' of England, France, and the U.S.A., but in the rising power of the U.S.S.R.

Eighteen years of Soviet power have shown that, to anyone who can face realities, all the material pre-requisites for a complete transformation of society are already in existence. It is not human wickedness in the abstract that prevents this transformation. It is the political power of the one class that stands to lose. Never in the whole of history has an obsolete order gone down without a violent struggle. And there is nothing in the least surprising about this, for a privileged class has its economists to show it that any other system of production is contemptibly inferior; it has its priests to show that any other system of morality is sinful; it has its critics and writers to show that any other system will mean the destruction of culture. It is true that in the period of crisis its theories are no longer self-consistent, no longer show the least connections with realities. But that does not matter very much. No class minds being inconsistent when the alternative is the realisation of the necessity of its own extinction. So naturally enough, the capitalist class fights like fury against its own overthrow, which is not only unprofitable, but also barbarous, sinful, and a guarantee of material and spiritual disaster.

The machinery by which capitalism maintains its rule is the State. The modern capitalist State machine is an instrument designed solely for the maintenance of existing property relations. It is obvious that where one class is oppressing another, any machinery which aims at the maintenance of 'law and order' is in fact a machinery for putting down the revolts of the oppressed, since the ruling class has no possible reason for disturbing the peace. It is only when two sections of the ruling class are at war with one another that one section will use the State against the other. And, even there, it handles the offenders with kid gloves. Compare the treatment of Clarence Hatry with that of an unemployed miner who 'steals' 6*d.* worth of coal. It is only necessary to look through any day's file of court cases to see that the present machinery of 'law and order' exists not to defend justice in the abstract, but a certain system of property relations. For instance, it is perfectly legal to starve, but for a starving person to help himself to a farthingsworth of a millionaire's property is a criminal offence.

If any proof is needed of the class character of the modern capitalist State, it is only necessary to refer to its activities during the General Strike. Looked at from a formal point of view, the General Strike was in its origin a sympathetic strike of the heavy industries in support of the struggle of the miners for a living wage, which the coal-owners could perfectly well have paid, if they had been prepared to surrender a fraction of their royalties and profits. However, they were not prepared to. The whole machinery of the State was mobilised to crush the strike. The strike was declared illegal. The police and the army were mobilised to protect the strike-breakers. Strikers were arrested, beaten up, imprisoned. On the fifth day a special ordinance was issued to the troops in action at the time, excusing them in advance for anyone whom they might happen to kill in the defence of order. Bourgeois members of Fascist and semi-Fascist organisations were armed against the workers. The capitalists gave the workers an excellent lesson in class war. They showed that, in the event of a serious attack on the sacred rights of private property, the whole State apparatus, king, lords, commons, judges, civil service, police, army, and navy, will be mobilised against the workers for any step, including civil war, that the profits of the ruling class require.

But it may be objected: all this took place because the General Strike was 'unconstitutional'; it is possible, provided you are very tactful, to take over control and make all necessary reforms by parliamentary democratic means. That is still the line of argument of the majority of the British working class. It is therefore necessary to examine more closely the nature of capitalist democracy.

It is perfectly true that at the time of its rise to power, at the time of its fight against the relics of feudalism, the bourgeoisie stood for an extension of democracy. At the time of the first Reform Bill, when the industrialists needed the support of the workers to wrest from the landed aristocracy a proportionate share in the control of the State, they developed a whole ideology of democracy. It is not so often remembered that the first Reform Bill was a purely bourgeois reform within very strict property limits, that, in the Chartist period that followed, the bourgeoisie were prepared to resort to civil war to resist universal suffrage, and that the subsequent Reform Bills were only enacted under very heavy pressure. Nevertheless, in the period of its expansion, capitalism stood for a certain limited democracy; in the first place, because after 1848 its power was never seriously challenged; in the second place, because it provided a safety-valve for working-class politics.

But all the same it kept in hand certain very strong safeguards, in case this limited democracy should ever touch its class rule. In the first place, the very possession of wealth gives it a powerful advantage. In any election campaign it has at its disposal the cinema and the Press on a scale with which a working-class party cannot compete. At a time of 'national emergency,' as in 1926 or 1931, it will also have the radio. A capitalist candidate can pay with ease the £150 deposit which is a serious burden for a worker candidate. He has at his disposal a fleet of cars and sums of propaganda money, with which, again, a worker candidate is unable to compete. And similarly on all questions such as the halls for propaganda meetings. In London the Conservatives or the Fascists can take the Albert Hall any time it amuses them. The largest hail in London available for the Communist Party is the Shoreditch Town Hall, and that it cannot afford very often.

Thus the whole machinery of parliamentary democracy, quite apart from the way in which the scales are weighted in favour of the backward county constituencies (more than three-quarters of the industrial workers' votes in less than half the seats) is built up in the interests of the party that has money to finance lavish propaganda. But apart from this there are very strong checks on the activities of Parliament. First of all there is the House of Lords, an unassailable stronghold of the reactionary property-holders. Secondly, there is the judiciary, at the present composed almost entirely of men who were previously notoriously reactionary in politics, who were scarcely able to fit the existence of trade unions into their legal theory at all, and who, right from the time of the Criminal Law Amendment Act, *via* the Taff Vale judgment and the Osborne judgment, to the decision that made the General Strike illegal, have shown a powerful anti-working-class bias. Thirdly, there is the Crown. Constitutional historians argue that, as the royal veto has not been used since the reign of Queen Anne, it is obsolete as an instrument to block the will of the people. That argument would hold water better if we had not seen the National Government so recently reviving legislation of the reign of Edward the Third against the leaders of the unemployed. Fourthly, there are the higher officials of the army, navy, police, and civil service, all of whom have very strong reasons for supporting the present order of society, and would not hesitate to use their position to thwart a legal attempt at Socialism. The army and navy officers take their oath of allegiance direct to the Crown. Fifthly, there is the whole machinery by which the rank and file of the military and civil services are separated from working-class politics. Recent articles by military authors show that officers of the army can use their position to do Fascist propaganda and get away with it every time. For a rank-and-file soldier to take part in revolutionary politics is a very serious offence. Sixth, there is the whole machinery of emergency legislation, by which if it pleases His Majesty to declare that a 'state of emergency' exists, every single democratic right can be at once suspended.

Thus the whole machinery of parliamentary democracy ensures that this democracy will only work in one direction. But, even though it is quite impossible to take power within this framework, the very restricted rights of capitalist democracy – right to hold meetings, right to a legal Press – sometimes become a check on the full, development of the capitalist offensive. So in that case open Fascism is introduced. The propagandists of the British Union of Fascists are never tired of pointing out that Mussolini formed a constitutional Government at the request of the king (though they do not emphasise so much the fact that Fascism's rise to power would have been impossible without the active support of the army command, and that the march to Rome was made in a sleeping-car). They are never tired of pointing out that Hitler assumed the chancellorship at the constitutional request of President Hindenburg, through the one loophole in the otherwise perfect Weimar Constitution. And they are right. Every capitalist constitution admits of the 'democratic' introduction of Fascism when necessary. In England the machinery already exists. If there is not yet an open rule of violence against the working class, it is solely because the capitalist class can manoeuvre well enough to maintain its power without it. As soon as its power is seriously threatened, the Emergency Powers Act and the Incitement to Disaffection Act will make short work of the remaining liberties of the English people. Thus the whole structure of capitalist rule eliminates the possibility of the peaceful conquest of power by the working class. If the working class ever wishes to take power, it must prepare for civil war. R. P. Dutt writes:

> Once you are in a fight, the choice of weapons depends on circumstances and your adversary. Civil war is simply the final most extreme form of the class struggle. Civil war is not a question of subjective choice; if it could be avoided every Socialist and Communist would make heavy sacrifices to avoid it, short

of the sacrifice which cannot be accepted under any conditions, the sacrifice of the working-class cause itself (which is the real meaning and inevitable result of the 'rejection' of civil war). In the words of the *First Manifesto of the Communist International*, 'Civil war is forced upon the working masses by their arch enemies.' (*Socialism and the Living Wage*, 1927)

It is not from any love of violence for its own sake that the Communists declare that it is necessary to prepare for civil war. The choice of weapons does not lie with them. The capitalist class repeatedly shows that it is prepared to adopt any form of violence rather than surrender its power and privilege. The fate of the dozens of constitutional 'Socialist' Governments – in Germany, Austria, Australia, Great Britain, Scandinavia, Spain, etc., not one of which has been able to introduce an atom of lasting Socialism, is the fate of the Socialists who 'reject' civil war. In the only country where the majority of the workers followed the line of the Communists, the result has been very different. The rule of the Hungarian Soviets is the only example in history where the working class was able, owing to the utter collapse of a war-defeated bourgeoisie, to come to power for a short time without a bloody struggle. But they only assumed power because the Communists had already made systematic preparations for civil war. And immediately after their victory they were forced into civil and international war to hold their power against the counter-revolution of the land-owners and industrialists backed with the armies and money of the Entente.

For the working class to take power by the existing machinery is impossible. And even if one were, like the Socialist League, the left of the English Labour Party, to make an assumption of this impossibility, even then it would still be necessary for the working class to shatter this machine and replace it by its own State form, for the whole structure of the capitalist State means that it is possible for it to work in only one direction, and for the construction of Socialism it would be both useless and dangerous. The savage repression which the working class has met, will meet, and is everywhere meeting to-day in its fight for power means that it is quite impossible for the workers, immediately on the assumption of power, to abolish the State, as the anarchists would like to see. If the working class is to maintain its power it will need a very powerful State machine in the early years of its rule. But right from the beginning it will be a higher type than the capitalist State.

The example of the Paris Commune is useful to show that the proletarian dictatorship is not a Russian phenomenon, that, in fact, it first originated in one of the Western 'democracies.'

These were the principal measures of the Commune:

(1) Army. The army for the first time became a genuine people's army. The standing army and conscription were abolished, and all citizens capable of bearing arms were free to enlist in the National Guard. (In the U.S.S.R. the continual threat of invasion has made it necessary to maintain a big standing army. But this army is distinguished from every other army in the world by the fact that its rank and file take an active part in politics, and no barriers are placed between the soldiers and the working classes. Moreover it is not the only armed force. A high proportion of the factory workers also are armed.)

(2) Bureaucracy. The wages of all officials were restricted to the same rates as the averagely well paid worker. In this way the danger of bureaucracy coming to have a separate and distinct class interest is guaranteed against. Every post was made elective, and every individual subject to instant recall.

(3) Judiciary. In the same way the judiciary was made elective, responsible, and subject to instant recall.

(4) Education. Every administrative post in the department of education was made elective. Education was removed from clerical control.

Thus in every sphere the Commune stood for an expansion of democracy, and the drawing of the greatest possible number of rank-and-file workers into the task of administration, the breaking down of the obsolete barrier between executive and legislative.

An examination of the Constitution of the U.S.S.R. shows a systematisation and an extension of these principles. The great historic contribution of the Russian revolutions of 1905 and 1917 was the development of the Soviet as the specific form of the working-class State. The Soviets (workers' councils, elected directly from factory and district units) combine in a single form all the advances made by the Paris Commune. The universality of the Soviet form was shown clearly in the revolutionary wave of 1917–21, when Soviets were formed not only in Russia, but in Finland, the Baltic States, Bavaria, Hungary, Canada (Winnipeg), etc. The Soviet revolution, led by the Communist Party, is now proving in China, even according to the admission of the London *Times*, the only form of government which can end the agrarian crisis and introduce stable government. The Soviet is not only the universal State form of the working class, it is also the highest form of democracy yet seen.

IX. The Pre-Conditions of Revolution

But a revolution does not make itself. Capitalism does not break down of its own accord and allow the working class to sweep effortlessly to power. The Russian revolution is often presented as due solely to the breakdown of the corrupt and inefficient old order under the strain of the war. A very slight acquaintance with the facts shows that this was not the case. The war breakdown greatly facilitated the victory of the revolution; but, unless the movement had been consciously planned, organised, and prepared in advance, it would not have had a more permanent success than the Austrian and German revolutions of 1918–19, or the Italian occupation of the factories. And the decisive factor in the preparation for a victorious revolution is the party. Lenin defines a revolutionary situation in the following terms:

> One must make sure, first, that all the class forces hostile to us have fallen into complete confusion, are sufficiently at loggerheads with each other, have sufficiently weakened themselves in a struggle beyond their capacity, to give us a chance of victory;

secondly, one must ensure that all the vacillating, wavering, unstable, intermediate elements – the petty bourgeoisie, and the petty bourgeois democracy, in contradistinction to the bourgeoisie – have sufficiently exposed themselves in the eyes of the people, and have disgraced themselves through their material bankruptcy; thirdly, one must have the feeling of the masses in favour of the most determined, unselfishly resolute, revolutionary action against the bourgeoisie.

Then, indeed, revolution is ripe; then, indeed, if we have correctly gauged all the conditions outlined above, and if we have chosen the moment rightly, our victory is assured. (V. I. Lenin, *Left-Wing Communism*)

Thus, under all circumstances, a disciplined revolutionary party, possessing complete confidence of wide masses of the working classes, with the ability to analyse clearly and react rapidly to every change in the situation, is a precondition of successful revolution. Chatterers like Wells who, without having studied Communist theory or practice, are fond of declaiming against Communists for their 'obsolete' propaganda of armed insurrection would do well to stop talking for a bit and study very carefully this and other passages from Lenin.

Not only the example of Germany and Austria, but the defeat of the revolution of European countries – Finland, Hungary, Italy, the Baltic States – immediately after the war, and the recent defeats in Austria and Spain, show that however good the objective possibilities are, without a powerful and experienced revolutionary party victory will be lost. In England in 1926, in Spain in 1931, in America during the early days of the Roosevelt administration, crises arose which, had the Communist Parties been as strong as were the Bolsheviks, or even as strong as the Communist Party of France today, could have been transformed into revolutionary crises. But the Communists were not strong enough and the opportunities passed.

Stalin defines clearly the objectives which the Communist Parties set themselves.

In order to be an effective vanguard, the party must be armed with a revolutionary theory, with a knowledge of the laws of the movement, of the laws of revolution. Lacking this, the party is not really fit to rally the proletariat for the fight, or to take over the function of leadership. The party is no true party if it limits its activities to a mere registration of the sufferings and thoughts of the toiling masses, if it is content to be dragged along in the wake of the 'spontaneous movement' of the masses, if it cannot overcome the inertia and political indifference of the masses, if it cannot rise superior to the transient interests of the proletariat, if it is incapable of inspiring the masses with a proletarian class consciousness. The party should march at the head of the working class; it should see further than the working class; it should lead the proletariat and not drag in the rear. (J. Stalin, *Leninism*, vol. I)

Without such a party the Russian revolution would have been impossible. Without such a party the revolution in the other countries will be impossible. To-day it is perhaps only true to say of the Communist Parties of France and China that they have reached this standard. But it is also possible to say that the Communist Parties of Germany, Japan, Austria, Poland, Bulgaria, Spain, Hungary, Czechoslovakia, Cuba, and Greece are on the way. Superficial observers in Great Britain are often misled by the relative weakness of the Communist Parties of Great Britain and the U.S.A. into believing that the Communist International is a negligible force (*see* the *Manchester Guardian* leader on the Stalin-Laval *communiqué*). There is no need here to produce arguments against these gentlemen. History itself will give them a very rude surprise.

I have attempted in this essay to outline a few salient points of Communist theory and Communist policy. It has been necessary to devote what may seem a disproportionate amount of space to the analysis of capitalist economic development and the capitalist State, because without such an analysis the Communist programme becomes unreal and unintelligible. For

Communism is not a scheme of social revolution according to an abstract scheme of what seems desirable, but according to existing realities, which are the realities of capitalism. If there are certain assertions without sufficient factual material behind them, that is not because Communists in general are dogmatic, but because there is not space here for a comprehensive study.

COMMUNISM IN THE UNIVERSITIES*

THE last few years have seen a considerable growth of Communist influence in the universities. That influence has often been over-estimated, particularly by the Right Wing Press after the Oxford motion. But none the less it persists and it is growing. It is no longer a phenomenon that can be dismissed as an outburst of transient youthful enthusiasm. It has established itself so firmly that any serious analysis of trends in the universities must take it into account.

This influence has shown itself in a steadily growing volume of left-wing activities. In 1933 the storm aroused by the famous Oxford 'King and Country' motion swept every university, and in the majority of Unions this motion was passed by a large margin. That same winter the students of Cambridge got themselves into the newspapers by an 11th November demonstration which successfully kept a three-mile march unbroken, fighting almost the whole way against students who were trying to break it up. In 1934 the Hunger Marchers received a great welcome from the students of Oxford and Cambridge. In 1935 the Northern Universities put themselves on the map when Sheffield students played a real part in the unemployment fight in February. For a few days Sheffield Communist students sold over 200 copies of the *Daily Worker* in a university of 800 students. At the end of 1935 it was significant how rapidly student opinion reacted to the Hoare-Laval plan. At very short notice big protest meetings were held at King's College, London, the London School of Economics, and Manchester. It would perhaps be true to say that the students reacted more quickly than any other organised body. Then at the beginning of this year the Federation of Student Societies, the revolutionary students' organisation, and the University Labour Federation formed a united body covering 2,000 students in all the universities. During all this period the membership of the Communist Party, though even now not very large, has grown steadily and continuously without once looking back.

Of course it would be wrong to represent this movement as wholly and solely the work of the Communist Party. But it is none the less true that everywhere the Communists have played a continuously active and leading part, and that the disciplined and centralised leadership of the Communist Party has given the movement a direction and co-ordination of which no other body would be capable.

Thus Communism in the universities is a serious force. It is serious because students do not easily or naturally become Communists. Communism has to fight down more prejudices, more traditions, more simple distortions of fact, than any other political organisation. It would not have gained ground without a serious appeal. Its significance is precisely this. It is the first systematic attempt by a working-class party to win over a whole section of the middle class. The Labour Party has made many efforts to adapt itself to middle-class prejudices. It has never made a serious attempt to win the middle classes into a fighting alliance with the Labour Movement on the basis of their own interests. That is what the Communist Party is just beginning to do. It is notable that the Central Committee of the Communist Party pays far more attention, gives far more criticism and more assistance, to the work of its student members than any other political body gives to its student section.

This swing to the Left has not come primarily because students are interested in politics in the abstract. It has come because the actual conditions of their lives, the actual problems with which they are confronted, force them steadily though hesitatingly to a revolutionary position. Because a student does not have to be interested in politics before he comes face to face with one great reality. The existence of the capitalist structure of society means that there is an ever-widening gap between the potentialities of science, technique, culture, and education, and their actual application in the world today. The most glaringly obvious form of this is the destruction of foodstuffs when people are hungry. But students for the most part are not yet hungry, and do not come up against this. But a medical student comes up against the fact, for example, that hundreds of children suffer every year from rickets, which is an unnecessary and preventable disease, simply because of poverty, and bad conditions, and the lack of adequate attention. An economic or an agricultural student will notice that the immense productive capacities of industry and agriculture are not being used – not because there is no need for industrial goods and foodstuffs, but because the capitalist property relations cannot overcome this widening gap. The whole field of British industry and agriculture today presents a picture of productive waste that capitalism cannot overcome, of preventable deaths and preventable accidents that are not prevented because no employer profits from preventing them, of preventable diseases that are not prevented because our present rulers find it more important to spend money on interest on war debt and on huge rearmament than on the health of the English people.

And this shows itself to the students in an increasing restriction of their possibilities in their future life. Already the professions are overstocked with qualified graduates. People with Firsts who, a few years ago, turned up their noses at teaching jobs are now glad enough to get a job in a secondary school. Medicos with first class qualifications will take the wretched job of a ship's doctor which they would not have touched not so long ago. I have known one case of a graduate with first class honours in Zoology with a job as a rat catcher at 30s. a week. Scientific papers have been printing advertisements for men with first class degrees at £125 a year. And the number of totally unemployed is mounting up: and unemployment for a middle-class person who does not sign on at a Labour Exchange results in a kind of hopelessness and isolation that is quite unique. The number of ex-students peddling vacuum cleaners and tooth paste for a living is mounting up. One point is worth bearing in mind. If during this upward movement, the 1935–36 'boom,' the professions are gradually becoming overstocked and saturated with qualified students – what will be the position when the next crash comes? It is not impossible that whole years of graduates will be 70–80 per cent. unemployed. The colossal nervous strain of competitive examinations on students who depend on the results for their whole future career means that even now a student's life is not so happy and carefree as is generally supposed. As to those who are just coming up to the universities to graduate, the outlook will be far more tough for them than it is for us now.

This general economic insecurity has its effects. Of course it does not of itself make revolutionaries. But ultimately all the secure prejudices and traditions of the English middle and professional classes depended on a stable and more or less well-provided environment. This comfortable life is breaking up, and with it the comfortable illusions which it fostered.

There is another process also at work. The developments of the post-war years have brought about revolutionary changes in the relation of every branch of knowledge to society. The official academic teaching is for the most part incapable of reaction to these developments, and is thus becoming more and more isolated from social reality. For instance, while the world economic crisis of 1929–32 was raging, the equilibrium economists of the London School of Economics did not find it necessary to bring forward any attempt at crisis analysis, and went on quite happily teaching the theory which explained why crisis did not and in the nature of things could not have a serious effect. It is not very surprising then that from that time certain students began to turn to Marxism, which had consistently predicted the crisis, and which had consistently based its analysis on the real world. To take another example. There is a course in the Cambridge History Tripos called The Theory of the Modern State. But in 1936 we are still being taught what was very 'up-to-date' in 1906. The course nowhere says what a Soviet is, nowhere makes room for an analysis of Fascism, is completely incapable of dealing with any modern political development. Is it then very surprising that students with a live interest in actual political developments should turn increasingly to Marxism, which alone can give a complete and self-consistent political analysis and a clear guide to action?

The same radicalisation infects to a growing extent all those students who are primarily interested in art and literature. And in the universities there are probably more people who read – and write – poetry and stories than in almost any other non-professional section. It is not primarily yet the superior ability of revolutionary writers – although when André Gide joins the Communist Party and E. M. Forster appears on an anti-Fascist platform it causes people to think. It is rather the feeling the society they live in has very little use for art or literature, and the increasing understanding that over in the U.S.S.R. the reverse is true. Only a few of the Soviet writers like Sholokhov and of the non-Russian Communist writers like André Malraux have as yet any big reputation. But what is increasingly significant is that whereas over here a writer has got to turn out slush if he is going to be a best seller, and a serious and advanced writer almost certainly cannot make a living from his books alone, precisely the contrary is true of Russia. The Russian literary market is immense and insatiable. A writer in England is extraordinarily lucky if his books sell 60,000 – it is quite an event. In Russia the number of novelists and poets (non-Communist as well as Communist) with sales over the 1,000,000 mark is considerable, and the number who circulate in the hundreds of thousands is very large indeed. The best of the Russian writers read their stories and poems to a meeting of hundreds of workers, where they are publicly discussed and criticised. And that seems quite usual in Russia. But the idea of T. S. Eliot or even left wingers like W. H. Auden reading their stuff to gatherings of miners or metal workers would seem ridiculous over here – so narrow and isolated is the literary public, and art so divorced from the lives and interests of the masses. But what more and more people realise is that in Russia the best of the writers are valued, encouraged, and assisted, in a way that contrasts startlingly with the official patronage of the Royal Academy and the Poet Laureate over here. And for those who are seriously concerned with the future of art, who feel, as more and more people feel, that if it is to have a future it must break out of its present isolation and irrelevance, this example is not without its influence.

Finally there are the direct political results of the crisis. Hatred and fear of war are very deeply rooted amongst the middle classes. If he wishes to get support for a rearmament programme, a Conservative has got to pretend that it is in order to preserve the peace, or he will not be listened to. Pacifism has had its deepest roots amongst the middle classes, to a far greater extent than in the more realistic working-class movement. But the fiasco of the disarmament conference cruelly extinguished any rosy illusions about a secure and easy path for peace under capitalism. And Manchuria and Mussolini's invasion of Abyssinia have provided a very convincing proof of the Communist thesis that wars arise out of the economic necessity forcing capitalist nations to imperial expansion. There is always a tendency amongst students to throw up their hands in horror, to talk about a world gone mad, to bury their heads in the sand and hope that the storm will miss them. But for those who are prepared to face the complexities of the situation, to face up to the dangers and difficulties in a realistic way, the revolutionary solution seems more and more necessary and inevitable. The next war will produce more Wilfred Owens and less Rupert Brookes. And here, too, the consistent and unwavering fight of the U.S.S.R. to preserve the peace at almost any cost, its willingness to make any concession for peace and its complete freedom from any aggressive aims, is contrasting more and more sharply with the military antics of the Fascist powers and the shiftiness and two-faced policies of the governments of 'democratic' Britain and France.

1933 marked the beginning of a big political change. The excesses of Hitler Fascism shocked and horrified the middle classes. It was not so much the attack on working-class organisations and working-class standards of living that affected them. It was the murderous persecution of the Jews, the Liberals, the leading scientists and writers, the wholesale destruction of democratic liberties. For a long time the Liberals fought manfully to hide from the reality and cried that Fascism and Communism were the same thing. But reality is proving too strong even for them. It is becoming more and more patently clear that Soviet Communism not only stands for peace but is winning all along the line on the economic front, whereas Fascism is heading for war and economic disaster. For a long time the cry still went up that they are both alike because there is no freedom. But even here the fog is dispersing. Publicists like Shaw, social investigators like the Webbs, have a considerable influence on the middle classes. And when both proclaim that the Soviet system is in certain respects the highest form of democracy yet seen, those students and intellectuals who are not too prejudiced to face reality at all begin slowly to revise their opinions.

And in every sphere the influence of the U.S.S.R. begins to make itself felt. It is not so much the economic victories. To a worker the fact that crisis and unemployment, that exploitation of class by class, have been wiped out, is far more significant than to a student, who in most cases has not felt personally the effects of economic crises. Unless he is a technician, statistics of production will not have for him the significance which they possess in fact. But the educational, cultural, and scientific successes of Socialism make a far deeper impression. And the Soviet fight for peace even more so. Now that the grim fight on the economic front has been decided, the life of the Soviets will seem a far more free, vigorous, and attractive life than ever it seemed five years ago.

Thus Communism is beginning to become a force in the universities, not because of any sudden wave of youthful romantic idealism (although in certain places that also plays its part), but because the very conditions of a student's life bring him up against a whole complex of problems to which only the revolutionaries are giving, or even attempting to give, a consistent solution. Of course the development is not easy or smooth. The middle classes do not surrender their comfortable illusions without a fight. There is a large section that is not yet faced with a decision, and will at all costs cling to the shreds of the 'independent' Liberal position, whilst they are sufficiently secure to blindfold themselves. And, of course, Communists often lose potential supporters by their own mistakes. Anti-Communist prejudices and traditions are so strong that to make any headway at all Communists must work hard and patiently: and they are damaged by any mistakes they make far more than any other political party is. The transformation of a worried intellectual into an effective member of a revolutionary party does not take place overnight. It is a long and sometimes a painful process. Thus nobody can say how quickly or how suddenly the Communist movement in the universities will develop. That depends on factors that are beyond anyone's control. But the foundations for a revolutionary movement exist, they exist in the very conditions of an ordinary student's life. It is very easy and to some people very comforting to sneer at youthful fanaticism. A movement so young as the Communist movement is inevitably at times naive, immature, over-enthusiastic, and provides a splendid field for the peddlers of second-hand witticisms. But it is none the less a serious movement. Out of the breakup of the standards of an entire class before changing conditions of life, a compact revolutionary core is being formed – a small minority still, but the most organised and efficient of the minorities. The changes that are going on now, often imperceptibly, but none the less steadily, will perhaps later assume a national importance that very few of the actors in the present small-scale events realise. But when the next crisis that will shake the whole system explodes, whether it is war crisis, economic crisis, or political crisis, the relatively quiet and petty developments of these pre-war, pre-crisis years will emerge in their real significance.

THE SITUATION IN CATALONIA

THE situation in Catalonia is more complex than in any other Spanish district. In this province, where the victory of the anti-Fascist forces is complete, where the social changes have been most extensive, the position is made extremely complicated by two factors: the tradition of Catalan national separatism and the anarchist leadership of the majority of the working class. This article is an attempt to disentangle some of the complexities. But, first, one reservation: my ignorance of Spanish has meant that the collection of information was not easy. Though I can vouch for the truth of every fact given here, and I have put down nothing which has not been thoroughly confirmed, it is possible that wrong inferences have been drawn, that some of the incidents which I believed were typical may have been exceptional. The future will show whether the analysis given is correct.

The Catalan Government
The present government is by a coalition of Republican Nationalist parties, headed by Companys and Casanovas. These groups and their leaders, jailed after the insurrection of October 1934, have two main points in their programme: democratic liberties and Catalan autonomy. They have also introduced progressive social legislation on the model of the Blum Government: 40-hour week, 25–50 per cent. reduction in rents, 15 per cent. wage increases; but most of these points are taken from the programmes of the workers' organisations in the People's Front and are not the real driving force of left republicanism. Thus we have a curious situation. At this early stage, the two main points in the Republican programme are already achieved. Democratic liberties have been secured; Catalan autonomy is a fact. Since 19th July the national question has been so rapidly solved that Catalan nationalism is now no longer an important political factor: there is no friction whatever with the Madrid Government; in the time of Primo Rivera most of the Catalans refused to speak Castilian, regarding it as

an oppressor's language, now it is almost as widely spoken as Catalan and everywhere gaining ground. Thus the Republican programme is achieved, but the Republicans are without a social programme that can meet the needs of the situation. The administration of the factories confiscated from Fascist employers, the solution of the hundred and one new problems in the villages: the organisation of a popular and democratic militia: the Republicans cannot cope with these tasks through the existing State machinery. The leadership is passing into the hands of the workers' organisations. It is not that there is any antagonism between the Republicans and the workers in spite of the efforts of the semi-Trotskyist P.O.U.M. (Partido Obrero d'Unificación Marxista) to break the People's Front, there has been no question of any serious political division. It is simply that the Republican programme has already been achieved: without a further social programme the Republicans are drifting on the stream and the real leadership has passed into the hands of the Central Committee of the anti-Fascist militia. Here the proportions six weeks ago were:

C.N.T. (Anarchist T.U.'s)	45 per cent.
Republicans	25 per cent.
U.G.T. (Socialist-Communist T.U.'s)	20 per cent.
P.O.U.M.	10 per cent.

It is possible since then that the proportions have been revised, since the U.G.T. is growing far more rapidly than any other organisation.

The Working-Class Parties

The *Anarchists* still have the support of the majority of the Barcelona workers. They have two organisations: the C.N.T., a mass trade union: the F.A.I., which is in fact a disciplined political party, but because the Anarchists refuse to recognise political action, it is called a cultural organisation. Their programme has been: libertarian communism, organisation of industry by the Trade Unions, power to be won by outbreaks of unplanned revolutionary violence. Thus their leadership of the working class has been a record of continual and disastrous defeats. But they have preserved their influence because in the past, in a country which under Primo was 83 per cent. illiterate, they have understood better than any other worker's party in Catalonia how to present their objectives clearly and simply: and they have fed the desire of the workers to struggle with continuous – though disastrous – action. Thus they have won to their ranks some of the finest, most courageous, most idealist of the Catalan workers.

Now great changes are taking place. In spite of their opposition to politics, this year the Anarchist workers voted solidly together in the elections. Step by step the old Anarchist Terrorist Utopianism is being driven back: by the growing strength and leadership of the united Communists and Socialists: by the magnificent responsibility and organising power of the workers in their own Trade Unions, who are more and more adopting, though not yet consciously, the line of the Communists and Socialists, and will not permit wrecking tactics by their leaders. It is a painful and difficult process: but step by step they are being forced to abandon their ideals before the realities of the struggle. Thus they still refuse to take part in the official government: and their pressure forced the Communist members of the Government to withdraw: but in fact on the C.C. of the militia they are assuming the responsibilities of Government. In words they will not recognise the need for discipline in their militia columns: but the realities of the war have forced the necessity of some kind of discipline on them: but they insist on calling it 'organised indiscipline.' The factories owned by C.N.T. Committees cooperate with Government representatives.

When the new Madrid Government was formed, there was a day or two of real trouble. The Anarchist leaders declared that the united front was formed on a tacit agreement that if there was to be any government it must be a weak government: and this strong Government was a breach of the united front. Some Communist workers in the C.N.T. were shot. (There is no doubt that some of the old underworld terrorists remain in the C.N.T.: but this shooting may also have been the work of Fascist gunmen sent into the C.N.T. as provocateurs: this is one of the few methods of struggle still open to the Catalan Fascists.) But then the Anarchist leaders must have realised that these tactics could only benefit the Fascists. They may have realised too that their own followers would not have supported any splitting tactics. In a day or two the opposition ceased. They gave their provisional support to the Government for the duration of the war.

When P.O.U.M. was carrying on its provocative campaign for the arming of every man, woman and child in Barcelona for 'the second revolution' at a time when all arms were wanted at the front, Durruti, the young leader of the strongest Anarchist column, telephoned back to Barcelona an order that has now become historic, for all Anarchist workers to send all sons to the front.

P.O.U.M. is a punishment for previous errors of the Communists and Socialists. Its leaders are mostly Communist renegades (like Oranin) and ex-Trotskyists like Andrew Nin. Before 19th July it was as strong as the Communist Party, and its Trade Unions were stronger than the reformist U.G.T. But the sweep of the workers into all revolutionary organisations has meant that hundreds of revolutionary workers have swept also into the ranks of P.O.U.M. For instance, Grossi, the leader of the second column of P.O.U.M., an Oviedo miner under sentence of death at the time of the elections, though he may be both reckless and theatrical, is without question a sincere and courageous revolutionary with a mass following. But in spite of divisions in the leadership, the dominant policy is provocative and utterly dangerous. It is a parody of the Bolshevik tactics of 1917: without taking into account that whilst Kerensky was carrying on an Imperialist war, Companys and Casanovas are fighting an anti-Fascist war. The opposition to the People's Front and proposal instead to form a workers' bloc at the elections would have driven the Republicans into the arms of the reactionaries; would have allowed the Lerroux Governments to continue in office: would have led the unarmed workers into struggle with the whole State machine. A further example of the pseudo-Bolshevism of P.O.U.M.: Budyenny organised cavalry in the Russian revolution. So what must P.O.U.M. do but organise cavalry too. They forgot that if Budyenny had had at his disposal roads in perfect working order and a fleet of fast lorries, he would not have organised cavalry but motorised columns instead. So the handsome young men of P.O.U.M. ride round the Barcelona bull-ring with flashing sabres and officiate splendidly as 'red Generals': but are not so useful at the front.

Fortunately, their influence is not growing dangerously. Their trade unions, a few months ago stronger than the U.G.T., have now very little influence, while the U.G.T. grows in a geometrical progression. Their militia is the worst organised on the Aragon front; even brave and intelligent leaders like Grossi are incapable of giving their troops proper political, military, or organisational training. Thus their splitting policy is no longer a serious danger. They have little left beyond their sectarian political leaders: a well-produced newspaper, *La Batalla*; and two to three thousand of the worst-organised militia; brave enough, but incapable of a real sustained offensive through sheer inefficiency.

P.S.U.C. (Partit Socialista Unificat de Catalunya) was formed from the fusion of the Communist and Socialist Parties with one or two smaller Socialist groupings. It has applied for affiliation to the Communist International. Before the fusion, neither party was strong. In Hernandez' discussion article for the Fifth Congress of the C.P. of Spain he states that out of 83,000 members of the C.P. in June only 2,000 were in Catalonia. There were only 10,000 members of the Socialist U.G.T. against hundreds of thousands in the C.N.T. Now after the fusion it is growing far more rapidly than any other party in strength and influence. U.G.T. is well past the 100,000 mark. On the factory committees in more and more of the big factories U.G.T. is equally represented with C.N.T., while the P.O.U.M. trade union federation, F.O.U.S., is practically unrepresented.

What is the reason for this phenomenal growth? It is that the Communists are winning universal recognition as the architects of unity, the initiators of the People's Front tactic, who alone made victory possible. All down the Rambla they are selling José Díaz' (Secretary of the C.P. of Spain) book, *Nuestra Bardera del Frente Popular*, beginning with the famous speech delivered in the Monumental Cinema at Madrid on the 2nd of June 1935, where, with the Lerroux-Gil Robles terror at its height, he openly claimed for the Communist Party full responsibility for the October insurrection and raised for the first time the slogan of a Popular Concentration drawing in the Republicans against the Fascists. It is only the unifying force of P.S.U.C. which can bring republicans, anarchists, police, and civil guards into a unified fighting force. It is no accident that a big section of the national-republican Estat Català is going over to P.S.U.C. It is no accident that the republican aircraft officers who remained loyal have picked their ground staff and technical services from P.S.U.C. It is no accident that the P.S.U.C. militia are incomparably the best organised and disciplined on the whole Aragon front. This union of Communists and Socialists has meant a thousand times more than a numerical increase in forces. This new party, though still in a minority, is more and more influencing the Anarchist workers towards a disciplined and responsible policy: its restraint is keeping the Republicans firm and loyal in the front, in spite of the profound social transformations which they did not see. It is showing to all the world that the fight to preserve all that is real and valuable in bourgeois democracy in Spain can develop logically, without discord between workers and middle-class Republicans, into a new and higher democracy, a new type of Socialist state machinery.

Of course there are still weaknesses. I have the impression that P.S.U.C. does not yet fully understand the special technique that is required for winning over Anarchist workers; that the Anarchist workers are approaching the Marxist position more from their own experience than because the propaganda amongst them is particularly effective. None the less, the idea of unity has gone a long way. The joint commission of U.G.T. and C.N.T. works continually to eliminate the difficulties between the two organisations. Although it is still too early to raise officially the question of organic unity, I have seen scribbled on the walls of a hospital: 'Neither C.N.T. nor U.G.T. – for a united trade union centre.' That is the way thousands of Anarchist workers are beginning to think.

P.S.U.C. is still a young party. Its constituent sections have far more experience of failure than of success. But it is showing that it can learn from its failures and grow in stature to meet the needs of the occasion. Workers who took out their party cards after 19th July are already rising to responsible positions. The tasks of the P.S.U.C. in Catalonia are in some ways harder than those of any other section of the party in Spain. If it can – and it is now alone of all organisations showing that it can – lead the struggle to success, organise the military defeat of Fascism and the political fight on two fronts against the vacillations of a section of the Republicans and the wrecking tactics of P.O.U.M. and a section of the Anarchists, if it can solve the question of Socialism without allowing the opening for anti-Communist intervention from abroad, without estranging the middle-class Republicans, and yet without lagging behind the terrific revolutionary urge of the workers, then it will have done a job of which the Bolsheviks of 1917 could be proud.

Industry

What is the position in the factories? In Catalonia at least the overwhelming majority of the big employers went over to the Fascists. Thus the question of Socialism was placed on the order of the day: as obviously no one was going to suggest the invention of a new ruling class to give the factories to. All factories in which the management had not returned by the 15th of August were confiscated. The workers took over. But the leading committees in the factories are not organised in quite the same way as the Russian soviets. The units of production are often so small and scattered, even in Barcelona – quite different from the industrial giants like Putilov in Petrograd – that to have directly elected workers' committees for all jobs is often impracticable. Instead, representatives are appointed, usually from the Trade Union, sometimes – in the villages for instance – from the parties. They have set about the reorganisation of industry rapidly and efficiently. The big Hispano-Suiza plant, with a long tradition of rotten management, is now for the first time working somewhere near capacity. General Motors is even more remarkable. It was an American-owned plant, but to avoid tax regulations had been transformed into a Spanish company. When the fighting started, Detroit cabled to close the factory. The decree was published ordering all employers to be back by the 15th of August. They didn't come, so the workers, here under Communist leadership, took over the plant. And they are running it as it hasn't been run before. When the Detroit management wished to switch over from the production of one model of car to another, the works were closed for a fortnight whilst the necessary preparations were made. Under workers' control the plant switched over, not from one model to another, but from car production to different kinds of war work in twenty-four hours without closing the factory at all. The first Stakhanovite group in Spain is already at work there – bringing to work in two months the concentrated experience of nineteen years of Russian Socialism. And at least in the factories where U.G.T. is strong there are none of the equalitarian difficulties which so troubled the early stages of the Russian revolution. The Spanish workers are showing how they can learn from other people's experiences.

The Middle Classes

In one sphere in particular the Spanish workers have a great advantage over the Russians. The nineteen years that have passed since October 1917 have made it far more possible for the workers to win over the technical and commercial middle classes. And they are not neglecting these tasks. Every week *Treball*, the daily paper of the P.S.U.C., carries articles addressed to these sections. C.A.D.C.I.*, the U.G.T. organisation of clerical and technical workers, is growing in strength and has the support of big sections of technical staff in the big factories. The Anarchist Syndicate of Liberal Professions every day reports the adhesion of new groups. Groups of small shopkeepers, waiters in smart restaurants where the boss has deserted, are beginning to run their business as cooperatives. Fortunately the rout of Fascism in Catalonia was so rapid that in a very few days everything was normal and production was proceeding: so there is no shortage of food or any of the essential consumption goods. The wonderfully rapid return to normality, for instance the opening of the cinemas (with 50 per cent. of the takings to the victims of Fascism) a fortnight after the armed struggle for Barcelona, all this has done a tremendous amount to keep the loyalty of the middle classes, to win their admiration and respect for the organising power of the workers; and in many cases the workers have won far more than respect, they have won loyal and active co-operation.

The Peasantry

In the countryside, support for the anti-Fascist struggle is almost complete. The big proprietors have everywhere deserted to the Fascists. Everywhere the peasants have elected Committees of the People to administer the abandoned estates and machinery. Rents are wiped out. The land is distributed by the committee, but the machines are used in common: at Sarinena, about 20 kilometres from Huesca, I saw four of the confiscated threshing-machines being worked. Each peasant brought his grain in turn, and the machines they all worked together. In the same town I saw a huge bonfire of title-deeds in the Market Square.

Rumours of all this must have reached behind the Fascist lines. Nothing the Fascists can promise, no threats, no atrocity stories, can keep the peasants in subjection. When Grossi's column occupied the little village of Lucueffa, 14 kilometres north of Saragossa, they found that even here, where no working-class organisation of any description existed, the Fascists had killed four peasants to 'maintain order.' One of the things I remember most vividly is how, when we marched into Tierz, 5 kilometres from Huesca, in spite of the fact that they had been deluged with stories of rape and atrocity by the retreating Fascists, the villagers came out into the Market Square to welcome us, and took us off to their houses where they had already prepared meals and beds in the straw. In one village we passed through, the People's Committee had taken a voluntary decision to continue paying their normal rents to the militia. The initiative shown by these committees has simplified extraordinarily the problem of obtaining supplies. The committees have mobilised enormous quantities of meat, and vegetables; thus the need to requisition supplies, which inevitably makes an army disliked, has been greatly reduced. A minor point, yet one that showed most clearly which side the peasantry's sympathies were on, was the calmness and discipline which all the men and nearly all the women showed during air attacks and bombardments. The peasantry have tasted freedom. Even if the Fascist forces should succeed in forcing their way farther into Aragon or into Catalonia they will have a very formidable enemy in the rear.

To sum up. The transformation to Socialism is proceeding in Catalonia. But it is not the melodramatic imitation of October, the 'second revolution' of the P.O.U.M., with Companys as Kerensky. The new state organs – the factory committees, the militia committees, the people's committees in the villages – are growing up alongside of and in defence of the republican democratic institutions. The Republicans can have no possible motive in obstructing the transition: the ruling class has gone over *en bloc* to the Fascists. Nobody, least of all Companys, is going to suggest that the Republicans invent a new ruling class. It is a classic demonstration to all the world that the defence of all that is genuine and valuable in republican democracy must, if it is to be successful, grow into a new and higher form of democracy, a democracy from which the peasants and middle classes have as much to gain as the workers.

The Military Position
The Forces on both sides. First, what are the forces at the disposal of the Fascists. Of the regular army of 116,000 officers and men,

perhaps 60 to 70 per cent. is still with the Fascists. About 10 per cent. is with the Republic. The rest has disappeared, returned to civil life. But, at least on the Aragon front, these troops are not reliable. In the Fascist Army they have to be forced into action by the battle police; they are already incapable of attacking, and at least one deserter I talked to declared that such was the fear of mutiny that in the Saragossa Barracks no groups of more than three are allowed to disarm together. In front of Huesca I saw a hundred of the deserters from the besieged hill town of Sietamo. What was impressive was not that they had deserted – hunger alone might have been responsible for that – but the way they did it. They brought their rifles and ammunition, the whole of the rifles of another company, two machine-guns, and an officer prisoner. I don't think any political work had been done amongst them; their chief motives were, hatred of their officers, unwillingness to fight fellow Catalans, and the terrible psychological strain of feeling the whole people against them.

Far more formidable is the foreign legion, 30,000 strong, and about 10,000 Moorish troops already in action. These are real soldiers, brave, cruel, and very difficult to win over, completely declassed. It was the foreign legion troops who were responsible for the capture of Irun. There are none of them yet in the Aragon front. If Bilbao falls and they can reach this front, the position will be very serious.

Then the armed Fascist formations, the Phalangists and the Popular Action will on occasion fight viciously enough on the defensive, but are more at home in their role as battle police. The Carlists in the north, however, are brave and disciplined troops, almost as formidable as the foreign legion. Political divisions are reported, how accurately I cannot confirm, between the different factions.

Finally the conscripts, at least on the Aragon front, are utterly useless: it is dangerous to arm them, and they desert at the first opportunity.

It is probably true, of course, that on the Aragon front the rebel troops are at their worst. They have lost the initiative, they are incapable of an offensive, and they are simply covering the offensive on Madrid. None of the best troops are in this front. None the less, reports from all fronts confirm that without immense foreign supplies of money and arms, the rebel forces would be in a state of disintegration quite early this winter.

Of the republican forces, I can only write of those on the Aragon front. Of the regular army, two sections remained predominantly loyal: the aircraft and the artillery. In both cases, the initiative came from the lower officers. Technically they were the best educated. It is possible too that they had a technician to the thousands of useless officers of the infantry regiments: the proportion of officers to men in the Spanish Army was nearly twice as high as in the French.

The police, the Guardia de Asalto, remained almost solidly loyal. It is not a very effective force, although it contains a good many unemployed workers who have taken it as the only possible job, and has more links with the working class than the army. At least these Storm Guards know how to handle a rifle.

The Civil Guard are the best soldiers in Spain. They were trained up by Primo Rivera as a special Fascist force, and lived under puritanically strict discipline. But Primo did his job too well. He had drilled them into such absolute loyalty to the Government that the majority remained loyal to the Republic after the 19th of July. But not without hesitation. In Barcelona they only came out of their barracks to join the Government forces when the fight had been won already. Thus the old Civil Guard has been dissolved and reorganised as the National Republican Guard. It is yet to be seen how they will fight at the front.

But of course the real forces are the workers anti-Fascist militia. Up to the present they have done practically all the fighting on the Aragon front. They are organised in columns by the different political parties – all of which send representatives to the C.C. of the militia. The unit of organisation is the century, with a century leader, divided into three sections of thirty, each with a section leader, each section divided into three groups of ten, each with a group leader. There are big difficulties in the transformation of the militia into a 100 per cent. effective force.

Their courage is incredible, but on this front they are not yet well enough organised to attack without heavy losses. There are some workers with experience of street-fighting, some who have been trained in political fighting organisations; but the number who have evaded military service is incredibly high – it is an army of anti-militarists. And with the shortage of ammunition, it is difficult to get enough rifle practice, and many must go into battle without being able to shoot accurately enough. Of the different parties the P.S.U.C. militia are far the best organised: Durruti has done something to teach his column 'organised indiscipline': P.O.U.M. is disgracefully organised.

At the moment, food, transport, and medical services are well organised. How they would stand the strain of a prolonged offensive I do not know. But in the present routine of the deadlock they are doing their jobs well – and lorry-drivers and doctors are worked far harder than anyone else at the front. Pay is good: every militiaman gets ten pesetas a day (worth £3, 10s. a week at Spanish prices): the money is raised at the factory where the worker was employed, and paid over to his dependants. There is no reason why this should not be continued for a very long time, particularly as the factories become more efficient.

The Aragon Front

The long front stretches right through Aragon, with the key towns, Jaca, Huesca, Saragossa, Teruel, in the hands of the rebels. The nature of the front is a string of villages and towns occupied by the militia with a network of outposts holding the hills in front. The front is so long that neither side can maintain a second line of defence. It is open warfare for the possession of villages and towns. So far the operations have been mainly confined to capturing village after village, driving the rebels right back on to the crucial line, the lateral railway that connects the four main towns on the front. But why is it, in spite of the superior morale, in spite of the fact that the rebels' best troops are not on this front, no decisive breakthrough has been achieved? This is an important question, for a break-through here would do more than anything else to relieve the pressure on Madrid. The answer is simple. These four towns control the mountain passes. It is impossible to get past them – a tactic often used before strong fortresses in the Russian Civil War – because of the mountains, high, waterless, making transport impossible. And it is impossible to take these places – with the possible exception of Huesca, without heavy artillery and aircraft: or at least possible only with hideous losses and at the risk of heavy defeat. And neutrality has effectively denied the anti-Fascist forces the arms which could crumble the Aragon front in a matter of days. Everywhere the position is the same: the Alcazar at Toledo held out for nine weeks, when a heavy bombardment could have made it enterable in a few days; 40,000 miners, the bravest troops on the Government side, are held up by a small garrison in Oviedo for the same reason; Granada and Cordova hold out because they cannot be bombarded. Supplies are pouring in to the rebels from Italy and Germany. The Sevilla aerodrome is stuffed with Nazi and Italian pilots. Even on the Aragon front, where the rebels are entirely on the defensive, and the main supplies are not sent, four Junker bombers have been operating all September. And meanwhile the militia have not even enough ammunition for proper rifle practice. I do not think the Fascists will ever succeed in subduing Spain: to do so they would have to wipe out a third of the population – which the Badajoz massacre shows they are ready to do; but the policy of 'neutrality' will prolong for months and even years a war that could speedily be ended. And if Madrid falls, though that will not end the war, it will enable the Fascists to set up a so-called government which Germany and Italy will rush to recognise.

Of course, there are organisational weaknesses at the front. A brand-new army cannot be perfectly organised in a few days. There is a real shortage of intermediate officers, heads of sections and groups with the necessary experience and authority. Thus military training proceeds under difficulties. Not all opportunities of conducting the war in an aggressive guerrilla way – raids, bombing parties, attacks on communications, etc.

– are being taken. But time and experience will bring about the necessary reorganisation. The example of organisation that the P.S.U.C. militia is beginning to set will take its effect. But reorganisation will not alone be sufficient to bring the war to a rapid end. Artillery and aircraft are needed.

The Role of Britain

There is deep resentment about the attitude taken up by the British Government. Even after the fighting was over, when the Anarchist paper, *Solidaridad Obrera*, was carrying a list of British businesses not to be interfered with, the British Consulate's stories of red terror were used to frighten the British residents out of Spain. All British subjects were ordered to leave; and many small business men who could now be in possession of their establishments were frightened out of their livelihood, because their businesses were confiscated when they had not returned by 15th August. There is strong feeling against the attitude of the British Ambassador remaining at Hendaye on the rebel side of the frontier when all the other important countries were being represented by their ambassadors at Madrid. Again, Barcelona workers are asking: in the first days of the fighting, when the newspaper correspondents of all the world were on their way to Barcelona, why did the correspondent of one of the most important British papers, who should have been on the job in Barcelona, board the first train out of the country and reappear in Burgos?

And it may be that Britain is not directly arming the rebels: but is the Government doing anything to stop the sending of arms to Italy and Portugal? Is it true that Vickers, Tyneside, are working overtime on rush orders from these two countries? Is it true that in the early days the British second-hand market was cleared of aeroplanes by agents who were in fact acting for these two countries? Is it true that Britain, which owns the Portuguese copper mines, banking, insurance, railways, electricity, tramways, whose fleet is allowed free access to Portuguese harbours, is doing all in its power to put pressure on its semi-colony to abandon help for the rebels? Or is the diplomatic pressure countered by quiet intimations to the Portuguese Fascists that nothing effective will be done? Britain runs Portugal. It could force the Portuguese Government into line without effort – if it wanted to. But as strong as the resentment against the pseudo-neutrality of the British Government is the interest taken in the activities of the British workers. The medical unit was received with enthusiasm. The Trafalgar Square meeting had full-page photos in the illustrated papers. The work of English militiamen like Nat Cohen, whose centuria captured five machine-guns in Mallorca, or the aviator on the Madrid front who brought down a Fascist plane, is real solidarity in action whose value is understood.

But at the same time, the T.U.C. decision for neutrality came as a heavy blow. It is not easy for Spanish workers to understand the T.U.C. block vote. And whilst they believe that the 3,000,000–50,000 vote represents the real feeling of the English workers, they will not set much store by resolutions of solidarity. And the attitude of the leaders who still oppose neutrality is incomprehensible to them. If Citrine and the English leaders who still keep the second and third internationals apart by the threat of splitting the international had any conception of the joy and enthusiasm with which international unity – even on the one issue of Spain – would be greeted by the workers in the factory and the militia at the front, only deliberate hostility to the Spanish workers' fight would allow them to persevere with their splitting tactics.

What is needed now is to redouble the campaign against neutrality. Money is wanted, medical stores are wanted. But above all, the fight against neutrality. We are now selling Harry Pollitt's pamphlet that deals with the stopping of the *Jolly George*. That pamphlet has a very immediate moral. If the dockers and transport workers to-day showed the same vigilance as they showed in 1920, I have no doubt they could avert shipment of arms to Italy and Portugal – destined for the Spanish rebels. This year we celebrated the tenth anniversary of our own great general strike. A great deal has happened since then: and I know the printing workers have a harder fight than before 1926. But if the London printers could put a stop to the lies of the Rothermere press, it would be a gesture the Spanish workers would never forget.

But again and again, it is the fight against neutrality that is most important of all. Give the Spanish Republic the arms it has a right to, and it can win in a few months. Continue the blockade, every day and every hour can be reckoned in the lives of Spanish militiamen uselessly wasted. The Government that was beaten on the Hoare-Laval Plan has not grown any stronger in 1936. It can be beaten on this issue of far greater importance. Now more than ever it is clear that internationalism is not a question of pious resolutions; it is an international fight against an international enemy. And if on their section of this world front the English Labour Movement can fight with one-tenth of the courage and determination that the Spanish workers are every day showing, it can perhaps play a decisive part in a decisive struggle.

Postscript on the Catalan National Question
Since returning from Spain, I have found Europe buzzing with rumours of antagonism between Barcelona and Madrid, of separatist tendencies on the part of the Anarchists. These rumours are not true, and are not benefiting the Spanish Republic. With the granting of autonomy, the Catalan National Question has been solved. There is no question of the Catalan forces acting in a separatist way against the Madrid government. Stories of the detention of troops and supplies in Barcelona destined for Madrid are being circulated. They are not true. Here are the facts. Some weeks before it was generally realised Madrid was in danger, the *Solidaridad Obrera* carried a leader emphasising the absolute importance of the defence of Madrid. As a result the 5,000 troops who evacuated Mallorca were at once transferred to the Madrid front. Every effort is being made to make Catalonia a base that can come to the help of every front in Spain that is in danger. But, quite correctly realising the unity of the war, the C.C. of the militia is concentrating its main drive on the Aragon front because a

break-through there would do more than anything else to ease the pressure on Madrid.

Further Postscript
Later news from Catalonia of the formation of a new government with the co-operation of the C.N.T., the P.S.U.C., and the Republicans. That is a fact of very great importance, if it is true. It means a very big stride towards the explicit acceptance of the Marxist position by the Anarchist workers. It means that the worst danger of division in the workers' ranks is at an end. From now on the problem of organisation, particularly military organisations, is simplified. The general tension arising from the dual control of the government and the C.C. of the militia is relaxed. Here is a government that can govern.

LETTERS

To Frances Cornford
Grafton House
Stowe School, Buckinghamshire

Dear Mother,

Thank you v. much for the letter. I was extremely interested to hear what you thought of Tennyson and Browning, as I am writing an essay on them. Personally I don't like either of them in the very slightest – I detest nearly all Browning and I am more annoyed by artificiality and Victorianism than I enjoy his occasional really good verses. (Don't say that I dislike Browning because I haven't read him, as I have just read almost all his poems except Paracelsus & Sordello, to try to find something which I thought was really good, but I was completely disappointed). My essay fails of course, because no-one can write a 5 page attack (for mine has not got to be less than 5 pages) without either quoting all the worst passages he can find (which I think is unfair) or else becoming tedious – unless he has got a very precise definition of poetry.

I have just come from a really superb argument with the School chaplain in which I defeated him rather heavily. The unfortunate man has to take us in 'Divinity' every week, in which we read a hopelessly incompetent book about the Christian religion, on which I and one or two others... attack him furiously. The good man is fairly intelligent but extremely slow, and it always ends by our forcing him to the most extravagant statements, or else loosing [*sic*] his temper. It is good fun, if rather brutal.

The Spectator are offering 10 gns for the best ghost story sent to them in a competition – fortunately for me of a very limited length. Mine is rather pointless and morbid, depending too much on an effect which it hasn't got, and I don't expect for a moment it will succeed. I will send it to you when it has been returned.

I have only one poem to send you this week – a very weak one, which is meant to convey the terrific and disorderly impression I obtained from reading Ezekiel – which, I think, must have been written under the influence of drugs, as some of the visions correspond so closely to the descriptions of mens visions under drugs. It fails rather badly – seeming somehow to be too obviously an imitation of I am not quite sure what.

Ezekiel Saw the Wheel

In the red depths of a hashish hell
   The wheels that are not what they seem
Smote in a vision Ezekiel
   Ran parallel across his dream.

In those fierce depths are flaming rocks
   An eagles head, and then a man,
A lions face and the face of an ox,
   Over against them the wheels ran

Above that waste of sulphurous stones
   Straight overhead, symbolic pain
Above the valley of dried bones
The wheels ran thro upper air.*

To Frances Cornford
Stowe

Dear Mother

Thank you so much for your letter. I have just finished reading the poems you told me to read in the letter before. I still cannot see anything in the Browning; but I understand, I think, why I ought to like Tennyson but yet do not. The Lotus Eaters – which you presumably meant when you said Ulysses? – I do like a good deal

   And round about the hut with faces pale
   Dark faces pale against the flame
   The mild eyed melancholy lotus eaters came.

That seems to me extremely good but poems like the Lady of Shalott put my teeth on edge.

Recently our English set had a competition as to who could find and quote the worst piece of English poetry. Mine was equal first

> The River dawdled silver clear,
>   A lane of mirrored sky
> Thro marsh and lawn of jewelled green
>   And restless fields of rye
> Thro haze and heat and round the feet
>   Of meadow sweet July.

The second prize was a verse from Browning. I can't remember it exactly, but the rhyme scheme was like this

> Explosive
> Strepitant
> Corrosive
> Crepitant
> O Sieve!

To Frances Cornford
Stowe

Dear Mother

Thanks so much for your letter. Have you yet heard the magnificent news yet? Sir Oswald Mosley (who is Reg's* favorite politician) & Aneurin Bevan, a Welsh miner and a bit of a poet have drawn up a manifesto for the Government in which they demand an emergency Cabinet of 5 to deal with the present state of affairs and the hopelessly incompetent government. I believe that the superb Mr. Maxton, for whom I have the greatest admiration as being a man of first class intellect and absolutely incorruptible is going to have a part in the cabinet. I sincerely hope so. If these people can get unemployment down there won't be the futile Tory majority at the next government. My only fear – and that a purely selfish one – is that they will anticipate the admirable scheme which I had worked out with Reg. We were going to collect a small but earnest band of enthusiasts who were to start from headquarters and travel round the country with great placards of DISARMAMENT, P.R. LIMITATION OF FRANCHISE, BIRTH CONTROL, NEW UPPER HOUSE, DESTRUCTION OF SLUMS etc writ large all over them. Then we would present a petition to the H of C demanding these things, signed by 10,000,000 people. If we did not get into power or get them to do these the undersigned would then cease to pay taxes, obey laws or do anything else, and you can't put 10,000,000 people in prison. In haste,

From Frances Cornford
Les Capucines
Glion sur Montreux [Switzerland]
5 Feb. 31

My dear John,

Thank you for one of the nicest & most interesting of letters. Do find time, if possible to write & send me the symbolic play. I should care greatly to see it. I have been writing an absurd piece of poetry all this morning – a song about tapestry,* which began practically in my sleep! If I don't feel it too absurd, when its cooled down & written out properly I'll send it along next week. I'm sure you've made an important discovery about slapping things down first of all in the rough – steaming straight ahead – & not letting the dragon of one's critical faculty get its head up – tho' it will be needed for all it's worth at a later stage. I sometimes write illegibly on purpose: so as not to become startled & self-conscious over my own words at the beginning. Judging from my letters I know it doesn't seem as if I need make much of an effort to do this! But when I once confessed *the idea of it in company, I was amused to find that Uncle Bernard** *did just the same. I am so glad you are writing about Flecker —* *(couldn't I also see his essay too, at the end of term?) I think your* *theory very interesting & very likely true — only I don't think it* *would be conscious — poets do these things, & critics find them out* *afterwards, & they're often right. But the poets do them without* *knowing that they are doing them. Only the poem 'comes like that',* *& if they try to alter it or regularize it, (which they are quite capable* *of doing technically) they feel at once something vital & precious* *has gone — tho' I imagine even the most intellectual of them mayn't* *know exactly what. You might say that the different Gates in the* *Damascus poems are different parts of man's nature which Flecker* *feels of very varying* importance — *& therefore one gate is so much* *larger & more weighted than the other. But perhaps that's only a* *mere superficial generalized way of putting what you've said. [...]*

To Frances Cornford
Stowe

[...]I hope you have liked the poem I sent you. I gave it Reg to criticize, and he was distinctly pro. It isn't particularly good. I have just finished the Jew of Malta. It is far better verse than Faustus, and far greater technical control, but somewhat futile in places and rather tiresome. I read it in bed this morning.

I remember last holidays your making some remark about Herrick being about the only poet who was good all thro. Recently I heard JHAS* on the wireless give him quite extravagant praise too. Why do you think he's so good? I have just been translating into later verse

'Whos that' cried I 'beats thee
    and troubles thus the sleepy.'
'Put off' said he 'all care
    and let not cocks then keep ye

For I a boy am who
    by moonless nights have swerved

and eek with rain wet through
and eek with cold & starved

I saw he had a bow
    and wings too that did shiver,
and looking down below
    I saw he had a quiver

That sort of stuff took about 2 minutes to write and even then
wasnt worth writing. It is reminiscent of Kensington Gardens
at its worst, only not so good. […]

*To Frances Cornford**
Stowe

The other day I was in Mr Spencer's rooms with CRS*, and
noticed a whole pile of letters in your handwriting on his table,
quite by accident ('Many too many,' Tristan said). I hope you
haven't been worrying yourself and him too much about CFC*
and me. He can't do anything about it, and it would be rather
ghastly if we became a positive nuisance to him. (If, as I hope,
he keeps all your old letters, and this was just a miscellaneous
assortment, I apologise for that remark.)

I have bought W. H. Auden's poems. The ones which I
can understand, which as yet are singularly few, seem to me
extremely good. But they are all difficult. I had rather fun
rewriting one of his easier poems as a romantic poem […]

From Frances Cornford
Les Capucines
20 Feb. 31

*[…] What an extraordinarily living picture of Marlboro' GMT**
gives. How strongly you feel his affection & admiration for the man
– tho' entirely 'this side idolatry'. I had always taken Macaulay's

black-washing view of Marlboro' without question. I know
Macaulay was able but how stupid he was too. Heavens how stupid.
No woman could be quite so stupid – they are all born knowing that
characters (& human relationships) are something so much more
complicated & subtle than that. (Tho' very few of them, till lately,
have put this knowledge into public words.)

I hope to get a poem done for the birthday too! Dadda asks me
to say that a copy of your symbolic play is what he'd like better than
anything from you. It will only arrive a couple of days late – do
send. Miss Miller has been abominably slow typing, or you should
have my Tapestry thing. Helena* has written the best poem she's
done yet. It is about a dance & a stranger. I want to send it along
to The Adelphi *or somewhere. Make her send it to you. Where*
did you get your T S Eliot interpretations? They are exciting. Can
Middleton M* really have been so upsetting in his life as that! ....
I think that London Bridge thing, – the trance – like feeling of it
– exceedingly good. I'm glad you're getting Graves. Do bring it out.
That verse seems to me perfect, & so true about children (to write
well of children or flowers is one of the hardest things on earth) But
I fear he might go & spoil it in the next verse by some carelessness or
arrogance. Some people take being an Artist, with a capital A, too
seriously, but he doesn't take it seriously enough, I think [...]

To Helena Cornford
Stowe
28 Feb. 31

Dear Helena

I have just finished reading your 'Intruder' that Mumma sent
me rather carefully. I agree that it is the best of your poems that
I have seen, and I should think the best you have written. I
always feel of you (& Edmund Blunden) that your best poems
are unwritten, and never will be. It seems to me that in this
case you were speaking rather as the prophet of the god de la
Mare, and that, though you were inspired, it was he and not

you that was speaking; that is why I dont like it very much, as I dont like him very much. The first line is just fine, but the 2nd strikes me as rather ludicrous. It calls up an impression of flesh coloured silk stockings and people dancing aimlessly without shoes. When I first read the 4th line I thought it was uneasy, which I think is better than unceasing. The second verse is very nearly good. The best part of the 1st 2 verses is the hot and cold contrast of 1 and 2 verses. I think that you would have strengthened that infinitely by a warm first line. However, that is impossible, from the poem. Flecker was the greatest master of contrast that I know of. Look at the 2nd sonnet of Bathrolaire. 'The dance he would not share' seems rather unnatural, as nobody had asked him to share it, but the tree line is very good. In the fourth and fifth lines the intruder ceases to be de la Marish and vague (thank God) and turns into definite William of Orange, and the one is evidently yourself. Did you realize that or not when you wrote it? The last verse I like too.

So much for the poem. I think the metre is utterly unsuitable for the poem because that metre can only convey one set of impressions at once, and very obviously you must have a sound of violins going on the whole time, though you have said that there was curtain between the dance and the window. What seems to me, though of course I cannot really tell, is that when you thought of the idea it seemd to you absolutely sublime, but that you weren't quite able to translate it into verse. Mumma said something about having it sent to the Adelphi. For Heaven's sake don't do that. The significance of the poem is purely personal, and it would seem utterly meaningless to the general public;

Love,

P.S. I am sending you this 'Alcibiades', though it is not ½ such a good poem as yours. Of the poetry you must judge for yourself, but the technique is a bad failure, except for the last three lines, which reproduce the onomatopoeia rather well. The diction (but not the theme) I owe nearly as much to Roy

Campbell as you do the diction and theme of the 1st 3 verses.
Write soon.

To Frances Cornford
Stowe
29 Feb. 31

Dear Mother,

What is the symbolic play? Am I supposed to be writing or
have written it, or is it a play of someone elses which I am in
possession of and what did I promise to do with it and how did
you know about it even if it did exist?

I read HDC's poem with interest, and I have sent her an
extremely detailed criticism of it, which she will no doubt
be rather annoyed with, as she will think I lay far too much
emphasis on the technique. It seemed to me to begin by being
just ordinary notbaddis [*sic*] WdLM*, and then suddenly it
changed into HDC and William*. Here it has a purely personal
interest, and you would be highly unwise to publish it. (If my
interpretation of it is not right, then it is utterly pointless and
less worthy to be published).

What an astonishing remark 'No woman could be so
stupid'! You wouldn't say things like that if you had read Agnes
Stricklands lives of the Queens of England, (I haven't either)
and the infamous remarks about John Skelton.

'It is affirmed that Skelton had been tutor to Henry... how
probable is it that the corruption imparted by this ribald and ill
living wretch laid the foundation for the royal pupils grossest
crimes!' Heavens, how stupid! And there is far more evidence
in the Merie Tales and the poems of Skelton, than there ever
was of Marlbrough [*sic*], whose character, judged solely by his
deeds, as Macaulay must have judged, is a pretty dirty grey.

I have just come to an end of the Robert Graves. I found
them exceedingly good, though intensely obscure. I dont think
youd like them a bit, as according to what I think your definition

of poetry is, you wont find them poetry at all. They are in his later and more intellectual style, and the simplest need a good deal of hard work, but all, at least all that I have so far been able to understand have been well worth it.

*To Frances Cornford**
Stowe

Dear Mumma,

I have just finished reading the 'Tapestry Song' which I did not like in the very least. I did not think it one-tenth as good as the 'Autumn Fantasia,' which I nearly liked. Jones paid it the highest compliment that he could ever pay to a modern poem (for he is tremendously traditionally Keatsshelleyish) by saying that he thought it was almost good.

I am sending you this poem not because I think you will like it, but if you think it is good enough please give it to Dadda for his birthday. Personally I am vaguely pleased with the earlier part, and I think it is the only thing that I have done that is worth keeping, but you won't like the theme or the language. Certainly I shan't attempt to get it published, or at any rate, not for a long time. The first half shows the influence of Roy Campbell and the second of T. S. Eliot very strongly indeed (not as strongly as HDC's poem had de la Mare all over it, and I think these two poets are immensely more important than de la Mare, whose collected works I have just finished reading...) The title is not yet decided.

> Who sits, deploring progress and Greek wars,
> Inventing poison gas and motor cars,
> With sun reflecting windows shut like doors,
> Schoolmaster, do not tell them to love flowers.
> Your inconsistency is plain to see:
> Flowers may have beauty, but not symmetry;
> Your truth's in an occasional felled tree.

The mathematical symbols of your brain
Can never understand what they explain,
So go with your kaleidoscopic books
At sunlight falling in the sparkling rock,
Yet even here you are not abstract – right,
Kaleidoscopes ignore the basic root.

This is the subtlety of your distress,
T[o fin]d an abstract truth and gain on peace: [...]

To Frances Cornford
Stowe
22 Mar. 31

Dear Mother,

Thanks extremely for your elaborate criticisms of the 2 poems. The rock poem wasnt the least bit genuine, and entirely insincere, as far as I am concerned. That's why I called it Alcibiades. You may show that other thing to all the people you want to, if you like. I disown it absolutely. It appears to me a complete failure in almost every respect. The metre is utterly unsuited to the subject, and very clumsily handled. I am sure that no sick man ever would behave in the least like that. There are 7 or 8 good lines which redeem the poem from being sheer drivel, but not enough to make it in the least good. Besides, it is almost a crib of Robert Graves' 'Down.' Do you know that brilliant poem. We must get his collected works. But I defend the last line. Obviously people, when they hear a bird singing above, naturally look up, and those after them look up to [*sic*]. It isn't really Richard Hughes*. I wrote that verse when I was only ½ awake, and it was something about railway lines and window blinds. Then I saw that wouldnt do, and had to alter it. I also defend the last line of Alcibiades. Obviously the 'deep' is a necessary part of the symbolism, & I think when it is read as a descriptive piece it is carried off by the pace of the metre. Or if they notice it it is as a transference of epithet [...]

To Frances Cornford
Stowe, 17 May 31

[...] As to my poem. I couldnt read ½ your questions, but as to this one anyhow. Of Course I chose a flower as being the most nearly symmetrical thing in nature, since a man with a kaleidoscopic mind would naturally choose it for that reason. But it is not wholly symmetrical, which is where he breaks down. So I don't think you can accuse that of a lack of commonsense. The alternation of rhyme and assonance is to express his uncertain self assurance. The schoolmaster trick of imposing doubtful views as accepted truths. That is why I have put 'Your truth's in an occasional felled tree' partly as a criticism of the worn schoolmaster axiom 'beauty is truth', instead of putting 'Your beauty's an etc'.

*To Sidney Schiff**
Stowe, 6 June 31

[...] I sympathize with you about your work. I too am in something of the same position: several times this term I have had a poem utterly ruined by not being able to write it down at once: and the mood is impossible to recapture. I suppose it is somewhat the same in prose writing but I have never yet tried seriously. [...]

From Frances Cornford
La Glycine, Blonay [Switzerland]
17 June 31

[...] I delight in your Dream Poem: I can make nothing of it. Can you??? But it is weighted with the sense of profound significance – like all proper dream poems. Helena came up yesterday & we laughed with delight over the fallen trees tendencies. I do hope youll write some more. [...]

Letters 133

To Frances Cornford
Stowe
[Sept. 1931]

[...] About myself: I should like you to consider rather seriously the idea of my leaving at the end of this term. Because I think that by doing so we should *(a)* save a certain amount of money. I don't know how much, but I shouldn't think CH* would cost as much as Stowe, even though I am a scholar. And all the inane expense of clothes would be cut down enormously; *(b)* that I think I should be able to learn as much or more than I do now in less time: and would leave myself a great deal more spare time to read and write what I wanted to. Also I might be able to make a certain amount of money from journalism of some kind: though that is very doubtful. My objection to Stowe is that I spend a good deal more time of the day than is necessary working and the day is so organised that I don't have time to do very much with my spare time. For instance on at least three days in the week, and generally more, I have to spend at least 2 hours of the day at rugger, which is a considerable waste of time because we cant do anything but concentrate on the game: and it is not enormously good as exercise, though not bad.

Also, rather important, since I have to be in bed by 10 o'clock here, which means altogether 9 hours in bed, since I need so little sleep I have to waste about two hours a day doing absolutely nothing, not even sleeping. In the summer I could read in the early morning but this term I can't. And obviously nothing can be done about that while I'm still here. Also I'm beginning to feel rather badly the need for interesting people: Heckstall Smith* is about the only person left I really want to see, and I can only see him occasionally. I think that what you said about the intellectual excitement of Stowe was true for me up to this term: but I think I have got all out of that I can, except for H. S., and I am distinctly bored by almost every one this term. I miss the intelligent people more than I had expected because I find that only by talking with them or writing can I ever really find out what I think about anything:

but I can't do either of those here. So I think that probably from these points of view it would be better for every one if I did leave. […]

I have just been reading Tchekoff's [*sic*] plays, *Uncle Vanya*, *Ivanov*, *The Sea Gull*, and I am very puzzled by them. The only thing I am perfectly definite about is that they are good, but how good I don't know. I liked *Ivanov* far better than the other two, but I was very puzzled by Ivanov's suicide at the end. It seemed to me untrue to the rest of the play, though possibly true to life. But then I am at present so puzzled by them that I am perfectly ready to believe I have misunderstood them from beginning to end. In the rather bad photograph at the beginning of the book he seems to have one of the most remarkable heads I have ever seen.

From Frances Cornford
Conduit Head, Madingley Road, Cambridge
9 Oct. 31

My very dear John, Thank you much for your letter. I do believe you will make a worthwhile affair of the rest of your time at Stowe (By the way can't you think out your writing when you wake early? Dostoievsky thought out the plots of 4 entire novels, I believe, in prison in Siberia.) and I believe you'll get a scholarship – & a good one – as soon as it's physically possible. And then have an adventurous time before the University (and at it) […]

To Frances Cornford
Stowe [Oct. 1931]

Thank you indeed for writing. I dont think you or FMC* either of you gave answer to the question I put in my last letter – probably because I expressed it so badly, as I didnt read it through. It seems to me that for me to leave would not be in any sense defeatist. If I left because I was unhappy then it would be: but I am not unhappy. Of course I dont enjoy it as much as the holidays, but it is perfectly tolerable. You seem to think that if I left it would be because I couldnt face certain difficulties: which is in a sense true, but it would only be a bad thing to leave if I couldnt face them because of some inferiority on my own part, which isnt the case. My difficulty is that owing to the arrangement of the school I find it impossible to find any outlet for all the energy I produce that isnt wholly wasteful. That I am not learning as much as I could at home for the amount of energy I spend. It does not seem to me to be in any sense my fault that I can find no conceivable solution to this difficulty while remaining at Stowe, nor does it seem to me in any way defeatist to leave in order to circumvent this difficulty. I think I have got everything I can out of this place, and that most of the rest of the time I spend here will be wasted. Also I think that you have always considerably exaggerated what Stowe has done for me. I think I always gain at least twice as much during the holidays than I do at Stowe. I think I might perfectly well be in much the same mental condition if I hadnt been there as I am now, though obviously not entirely. I have gained a good deal, but I dont think there is much more I can get out of it.

If, therefore, it is not defeatist for me to leave, the question I want you to answer is Surely if I can learn more and at the same time enjoy life more and save money by working at home, oughtnt I to be there?

In haste

From Frances Cornford
Conduit Head
23 Oct. 31

[...] Old Schjff writes that he's been much troubled with financial family affairs – that he's treated you shabbily about not writing – & that it's weighed on him – that he is going to write (of course I'm going to tell him not to hurry) 'His last letter to me, very difficult to read & some illegible, lies on my table unanswered. What a pity he

does not reform his writing while there is yet time. It is a recurrent shame to me that my own is so abominable' His own is difficult sometimes – isn't it? from its curious, cramped quality? But it is always painstaking. It is never a scrawl, which sometimes has a suggestion of rudeness in it, as yours has – though Im sure this isn't intentional. But it gives the impression the reader isnt worth taking ordinary trouble for. And when the reader is distinguished & elderly like dear old Schiff, it makes me sad. I know you & I both have a certain amount of Darwin hand-clumsiness to contend with, but I do think this can be conquered even at 45 – and I do mean to try. I think what happened to you was this? You had a quite legible writing as a small boy. Then came the time when you wanted to go much quicker, & this coincided with the sense that an indistinct small scrawly writing was much more adult. So now the scrawling habit has gone down into your unconscious & it's much the easiest. It will be an effort till a legible habit gets down there, but there it will be for the rest of your life. I know I have got a beam in my own eye, & live in a glass house – but I dont think it prevents what I say being true [...]

From Frances Cornford
Conduit Head
24 Nov. 31

[...] doubtless there are grave scandals at Stowe – only there are equally grave scandals everywhere. *There are in the way I conduct my household & above all in my own psychological makeup. One, I realize, is a trait I've transmitted to all of you, in varying forms according to your different temperaments and that is a sense that one somehow has an inalienable right to be doing what's most interesting to oneself & most important all the time – with a corresponding sense of injury when one isn't. On Sunday HDC didn't want to go in the afternoon & play Bach at the Hugh Stewarts* – tho' Dadda wanted her to go with him. I said what I thought, that as she was really tired, she'd much better stay and sleep. She said: 'It seems such a shame when Dadda is always doing what he doesn't want to do,*

that I shouldn't just this once.' I found myself saying with some vehemence, & to my own surprise that everybody in this family, including Dadda, were nearly always doing what they wanted to do most – far more than nearly all the rest of the world – & we all made a good deal of fuss when we couldn't. It is glorious to be a man of learning, as my father was, so that your work is what you most want to do. But it can be a spoiling atmosphere. [It certainly was for me, plus being an only child, & being convinced I was destined to be an artist.] (Tho I don't mean Dadda's spoilt.) When I think of the bus-drivers and asylum attendants & shop assistants & what-nots of the world. I know that later my life must lead me among more such, to shake me into proportion – you remember my ancient music-hall song? ending:

> *But what's the matter*
> *With Saturday-aturday*
> *After-nune?*

I don't think it's too Chestertonian of me to think it's gallant & sane. I suppose one can say that the cockney has to be a shop assistant to earn, & therefore necessity makes him make the best of it, & of his one half holiday for himself, whereas it isn't really necessary for you to be at Stowe – But as we can none of us think of a better place for you to be in at the moment – It comes to the same thing as necessity, 'that blessed Necessity', though I can see it's very hard it should feel like it. [I am sure it was not army discipline, as has sometimes been said, but the restfulness of complete necessity, that made unexpected people like Edward Thomas & Ben Keeling so happy at first in the army.] I also think that Beauty & the Beast is one of the most profound allegories & applies to you & Stowe – and all you completely detached critics of Stowe.

I allowed myself a walk in the sun this morning, & scribbled my thoughts chaotically under a haystack. They apply probably more to my own problems & my wish to clear up my own vision of things – more than to anything you wrote. But I'd rather send them along just as they came.

[…] We went and heard Prince Mirsky last Sunday night on Dialectical Materialism – the philosophy of Communism. I longed

for you to be there. Haldane tackling him. But Esther* made much the best speech & Dadda asked much the best question, which really drew him. I'll have to tell you about it at length. Mirsky can't think much – but he looks like a Byzantine Saint & he believes in Communism like a B.S in the Trinity – And his smile, when his ugly black-bearded face lights up with belief & hope, is one of the best things I've seen for ages. […]

To Frances Cornford
Stowe

[…] About untidiness. The stage I object to is when a room gets so untidy that one can't find where anything is. I dont mind things getting out of place and dusty, as long as I can find them as soon as I want them. For instance I dont (as you do) mind books lying crooked open and shut on tables, as long as I know where each one is. I dont believe chaos begins till things get lost.

[…] I feel more and more strongly that I oughtnt to be doing history: I really begin to regret not having taken up English. Philip Gell has far more interesting work than I have; Tristan had, too. I think your prejudice against it isnt altogether justified: I wish I could send you some of CRS' questions: it seems to be the only subject which gives you a chance to do a good deal of thinking on your own. At History I do a good deal of work on my own, but for all ideas (since the period covered is so vast) I simply have to pick other people's brains. But it is far too late for me to change now.

From Frances Cornford
Conduit Head
27 Nov. 31

[…] Surely nobody at fifteen can hope to be doing really original work? You must get a grasp of your whole field first. FMC says that

he did not (or ever dreamed that he could) begin any really original work till he was about 25. Surely in either subject all one can do is to react originally. I mean when you were quite a small boy & I asked you what you were thinking about & you said: – 'Whether O Cromwell was really *sincere' or that you were wondering what Napoleon could have done for France, if he'd cared more about France than himself – those were really original reactions. […] I feel you are wanting something too soon. This seems to me to fit into what I wrote about the unconscious demanding-too-muchness of all of us in this family.*

There's another thing which has always struck me. You are a born generous person & you accept human relationships (not only the ones you've freely made – but also those which Fate has chucked you into) as naturally involving a system of give & take. It doesn't in the least matter in how odd or wrong a stage is the human being with whom you have a relationship. I mean you feel it ugly & cold blooded to say:- 'I've got all I can get out of Hutch, now', for instance. To me places – institutions like Stowe – are alive too. Not so alive as an individual, but still there is something ugly & cold blooded about only criticizing destructively & taking. I don't think in practice this is all you do – But it is all you intend theoretically. I often wonder why Communism, which means giving so much more *(far more than I can envisage doing) to an institution attracts you so much? But these most hasty reflections must catch the post.*

To Frances Cornford
Stowe
[Autumn 1931]

[…] By 'original work' (did I really use that word or did you misinterpret me) I only mean work that enables one to use one's own mind instead of picking other people's brains. Of course I didn't mean anything so ludicrous as work that hadn't been done by anyone before. But at present I do all work here by a kind of formula: and the period to be covered is so idiotically great that it's the only thing I can do. I don't claim to be able to make a Cuvier-like reconstruction of character from the limited selection of badly chosen facts that one has at one's disposal. And I haven't the hero-worship or sentimental reverence of the past like Helena. [...]

From Frances Cornford
Seabourne, Marine Close
West Worthing [Sussex]
Fri. night. [Jan. 1932]

[...] I also much hope that you will type at least *the notes of your TSE thing, as it would really interest me to see them, very much. Will you type a poem for me – which you will deeply disapprove. And so do I, though not its conception – It contains the purely conventional shepherd – who you would think inadmissable – & I feel as free to take him as Sir P Sidney or Horace might, only in this case he hasn't come* off. *I think he's mixed up with much too realistic Swiss scenery. Also the irregular rhyming metre has failed. It was meant to represent recitative in music, mixed with bits of typical melody. But if I could get it a little better I might try it on the old* Spectator. *Heaven knows I've worked hours enough (though so unsuccessfully) at straightening it out.*

To Frances Cornford
Stowe
[Jan. 1932]

[...] I will send you my Eliot essay when CRS has finished with it as long as you can manage to send it back in time. You wont like it. It begins with a few rather wild generalizations about symbols and meaning – subjects which I am quite incompetent to deal with: that part I have finished: and goes on to a critical abuse of McGreevy [*sic*]*, which I am much more competent to do, and enjoy writing a lot. How it will end I dont know. [...]

To Frances Cornford
[Stowe]

[...] the shorter poem ... I liked – except for 'coloured' lights
– if you stress the fact that they were coloured, surely you can't
avoid associations with decorative lights – magic lanterns etc,
which I don't think you intended – certainly it isnt consistent
with the rest of the poem, or rather my interpretation of the
rest of it. It reminded me strongly of an equally short poem by
Herbert Read, which I have always liked. (NIGHT) [...]

At present I feel more and more strongly inclined to do
English: certainly at present all my interest is their [*sic*]. It
seems to me that the main object of doing history is for the
research historian, which I certainly dont intend to be: even if,
as you think, I will end up by doing history, it will be applying
new theories to the facts; I dont think I should ever be able to
narrow my interests enough to be able to spare the time to do
research work. And till there is some theory I want to prove by
history, or something I want to discover, there seems very little
point in continuing writing essays on the 'Domestic Reforms
of Charles V' and the Balance of Power in the 18th century
etc etc when all my interests are elsewhere. Besides, through
English I can indirectly approach psychology and the whole
problem of language: and while at history I feel quite incapable
of doing sensible work for a silly question – because to find
anything new one has to do infinitely more research work than
I shall be able to – while at English it is perfectly possible. That
is at any rate what I feel at present. [...]

From Frances Cornford
Conduit Head
24 Mar. 32

[...] HDC says Matachin *is you. If so Hooray. Anyway I think it
far* the best *& a really moving piece of work – especially the end. I
think it very good. [...]*

Your criticism of my poem is v. sound. I'd thought of it. But I must keep the coloured *because of the element of hoping phantasy in the woman's mind. First of all I saw her at a square window looking down over a little seaside town with a pier – which would have made it outwardly right and then it got more countrified. […]*

To Frances Cornford
Stowe

Here are your two poems. I don't like either of them as much as the previous short one: though I think that in both of them you are getting much closer than in any of your earlier poems – except a few lines now and again – to a live language. But in the first, 'as it tells the birds' grated on me at any rate unpleasantly. They seem to be utterly false to the image-structure of the poem, which is surely as important as the music of it. I wonder, how much of your poetry is shaped by tradition: are the poems that you write really your most important experiences? or has your view of poetry been so much moulded by the traditional view that the more important experiences are too repressed to occur in poem-form at all? I don't know in the least myself: but it always seems to me that you have a great deal that needs to be said more urgently but can't because of the limitations of your view of poetry – because I should guess (though I don't know) that until fairly recently you would have denied (and perhaps still do) that every subject is equally 'poetical.' It may be, of course, that I am trying to substitute another and equally narrow concept of poetry; but I think it can include all that yours could and more besides – though I think that language is fantastically limited at present, and the more psychology I read the more I am convinced in this: in short I believe in a much stricter vocabulary and a much wider range of subjects: and writing unselfconsciously on a subject enormously depends on whether anyone else has before. To say something not only new, but that will enforce in most readers, if they are to accept it, an extended definition of poetry, is almost impossible to do without some sort of flourish and defiance of the stupider reader in advance: it is there that tradition is so important, that your tradition has gone so utterly wrong.

To Frances Cornford
Stowe
[June 1932]

Halfterm at last. I have done and thought so little for the past month that theres very little to say. Not a good half, but I have at least learnt a little more history than I usually do, which is something. I think that coming into contact with new minds is about the most important stimulus there is for anyone who cant in the normal course of events find enough to do. My trouble here is precisely the opposite of Xopher's: I can get through a whole day without having to make a single new response of any kind to a new situation: everything done before. I suppose the meeting of new people is interesting because it provides your new mind a situation that makes a full response possible: but one cant concentrate on anything that can be done without concentration. Curiously everyone else is feeling just the same stagnation as I am now. Partly perhaps the flatness and dullness of the country: I was far more alive in Switzerland than Nice.

Fortunately the bathing is very good here: now I have finished with critic [*sic*] I get most of the afternoon free down at the lake, which makes a good deal of difference.

I am still no nearer deciding what to do at Cambridge. At present theres no hurry but I wish I had some sort of inclination either way.

To Frances Cornford
Stowe
10 July 32

[...] The need for a revolution with fighting. I think all that is needed is enough force to hold up communications – telegraph besides roads and rails – and get wireless stations and newspaper offices. Army must be managed with fairly clever moderate propaganda. After that all fighting would simply be a function of the enemy resistance: first measure to divert unemployed would be to collectivise Norfolk farms (I think the only thing that would make them pay). But the more I read of party politics, the more I despair of a constitutional success: an election-organised party could never do it. I think English moderateness and compromising is largely a result of many years' prosperity – though of course there are racial and climatic reasons as well. I think anyone will fight when they have been hungry long enough – as we will certainly have to do sooner or later while capitalism continues. Between the Napoleonic wars and the Victorian prosperity the workers were only kept down by force from above and by a hopeless lack of organisation on their part: the history of that part of the century is fairly grim reading – Gordon riots, Luddite riots, Peterloo massacre, etc. And I think the longer they are kept down, the nastier the actual outbreak will be: better to control and organise it from the start. There really needn't be much fighting as (if people are sensible) there are so very few people to fight against. [...]

To Tristan Jones
Stowe
26 July 32

I have been listening to more and more music lately, and I am beginning to work out a sort of elementary musical theory, though that depends mostly at present on the extension of an analogy from a definition of poetry I have been at work on for some time. I wish I knew a whole lot more neurology. Talking to Joe Henderson* and my mother one forgets that there is anything in psychology behind dream-analysis, because it is so much more interesting than the purely mechanical reflex business; but I shall soon find it essential to learn a lot more of that if I am to know what I am talking about at all. I am beginning to see the significance of a musical general rhythm; but the effect of a tune completely baffles me. I think quite a good thing for me to do when I leave here would be for the first three months or so to learn up all the theory of music there is up to date, and all the technical side which I know nothing whatever about yet.

With luck your introductions *[to people in Moscow]* ought to help you a good deal to see what actually is happening. I should think that if the tour only goes officially round the show places, they'd be able to tell you where you could see what was actually happening. I think the difficulty of trusting most post-war books about the USSR is that writers seldom (except statistically) contrast the present with the pre-war conditions (which must be the only fair test) but judge them by Western European standards, and decide there's a good deal more hardship than there actually is, hardship being, I suppose, purely relative to the mental conditioning of people, at any rate up to a point.

Write an account of – at – from – Moscow if you have time; it will be amazingly interesting to find out what it really is like. How I envy you.

To Frances Cornford
[Stowe]
[Sept. 1932]

[…] Living independently for me will be a big experience, as I haven't yet done that or anything like it, and before I can find the really sensible normal way of living and working I should try a number of ways that wouldn't work; which would be a nuisance to anyone living with me. You see I have lived so long in institutions (and with a family) that I shall react violently against any sort of routine for a while until I have solved my own. Also, I am now (though of course that doesn't mean that I shall be then) particularly anxious to be alone for a while. I feel you are partly anxious that I should be with a 'responsible' person for the first few months; but I really don't think you need worry. I know myself when I am living the right sort of life; the silly things I have done in the past were because I haven't yet begun to find the right organisation of life. I am working at a subject which doesn't greatly interest me here under very restricting conditions and at home I haven't (and obviously can't have) to indulge the accumulated reaction against the petty interferences that are going on at school.

I have bought myself a *Kapital* and a good deal of commentary on it, which I hope to find time to tackle this term. Also the *Communist Manifesto*, with which I was a little disappointed, though part of it was an extremely remarkable prophecy. Also a pamphlet, *Wage Labour and Capital* (only 50pp., do buy it and read it with FMC if ever you have time, as it is perfectly intelligible) which is (I think) a summary of the economic argument of *Kapital*. Most of Laski's criticism would seem to be directed against Engels' introduction. I found nothing whatever to quarrel with in the main thesis of Marx's own section. It seems to me dishonest for men like Laski to dismiss the Marxist interpretation of history and yet proclaim Marx as a great prophet, because his wonderfully accurate prophecy is dependent on his interpretation of history. Where it seems to me that he went wrong is in applying terms like the class-struggle (which is a legitimate abbreviation of what actually happens) as the whole and simple truth. It's far more complicated than he seemed to realise. But I believe that in this, too, his limitations are important in making him intelligible.

Do you know anything of R. Palme Dutt? I have recently read a brilliant attack by him against the I.C.I.* in the *Labour Monthly*, and a very good article on 'Intellectuals and Communism' in the *Communist Review*. He is extraordinarily intelligent but almost equally bitter.

I have found it a great relief to stop pretending to be an artist; and in my reaction against over-estimating all forms of art for so long I am going through a period of complete contempt for all artists; which I don't suppose will last long. [...]

From Frances Cornford
29 Sept. [32]

[...] I have spent this week reading the Greek anthology with profound admiration, in order to bully FMC to quoting some of it in his next talk – (which I think will be far the most exciting of the 3) I feel as if I could read it forever. I also woke up last night & wrote a poem – Alas how unlike those in the Greek anthology. It was after reading Dorothy Wordsworth's journal – but this roused a mood I have often acutely felt before. You can call the poem indifferently (till I get the right name) Biography History The Autonomous Complex *or* Unannealled

> *When we would reach the anguish of the dead,*
> *Whose bones alone, irrelevant, are dust,*
> *Does it not seem as though we must, we must*
> *To some obscure but ever-bleeding thing,*
> *Unsatisfied, our needed solace bring?*
> *(Like a resolving chord, like daylight shed.)*
>
> *Or through thick time must we reach back in rain*
> *To inaccessible pain?*

I must say I rather agree with you about artists. Or rather the intolerable way they take themselves so seriously as artists *(for in another way I don't think life would be worth living without them.) I don't think the greatest people of this age are artists. The most* important *kind of creativeness doesn't seem to be taking that form. An artist of a really great stature (such as I consider Tolstoy) was far too occupied in the terrificness of living to take himself seriously in the modern way.*

Nor do I think in thus agreeing with you that you have the temperament of an artist (Here I begin wondering what do I really mean by an artist?) At least I used not to think so when you were small. But perhaps it is dangerous now to hark back to the past, when human psyches have such an infinite power of change & development.

But I remember thinking for instance, when Xopher cried out to stop me singing Lord Rendal because it was 'too terrible' and you said 'You are silly, Christopher, when you know *Lord Rendal wasn't a real person.' — that that wasn't a distinction that would naturally occur to an artist. And yet the power to make it meant something remarkable in another way.*

Certainly we'll get that shorter Marx thing & read it. Keep the things by the bitter brilliant man for us to read too when we come to Stowe, if they're in periodicals of your own?

We're reading Maxton on Lenin but of that next time. [...]

To Frances Cornford*
Stowe
[1932]

[...] I don't know whether or not I like your poem; or rather whether or not I understand it; because words seem to have a totally different meaning for us. I can only understand what you are saying because I know you personally even in your letters; that is, they would mean something totally different from what they do if I were to read them without knowing you, say in some collection of letters.[...]

To Frances Cornford*
Stowe [1932]

[...] Last holidays you said to me that the most any poet can do is to write a few individual lines for himself in every poem and let the tradition he writes in write the rest for him (or words to that effect). For poets writing just after a revival of tradition this seems to be all right; but for poets in the decadence of a tradition it is impossible. (Could the poets of the Romantic Revival have let the tradition of Pope and Dryden communicate for them?) and this age seems to me just such an age of decadence of tradition. Notice that Eliot and Graves both write so carefully that hardly a line of either of them could be confused with another poet; and they have to do this because they are building a tradition. [...]

To Frances Cornford*
Stowe
[1932]

[...] I always think that writing about poets you always overestimate the importance of the individual in determining what he is going to write. It seems to me that every line anyone writes must be influenced by a host of fairly clear economic, political, literary factors and innumerable obscure more personal factors entirely beyond the poet's control. And therefore that the self-conscious building of a tradition is important. For instance, I remember that you once said that when you first read it, Browning's 'blue spirit of a lighted match' seemed to you a very daring line: if it seemed daring to you, then it is pretty clear you couldn't have written a line like that yourself without being selfconscious. And since poetry ought to be written equally unselfconsciously on every conceivable attitude to every conceivable subject, the original founders of a tradition have to use such symbols and phrases and subjects deliberately and defiantly, so that their successors can write a freer type of poem after them. Thus: thanks to Eliot and Graves I think I am able to tackle a far wider range of subjects in a more direct way than you were when you were at the same stage as I am. But there are still a number of poems which I have in my head intrinsically as good as any other, which, because of the history of poetry during the last ten years, I can't and never will be able to write. And my attitude to certain subjects, if I am going to express it as a poem at all, is predetermined by what has come before: I think it was the same in every age, except perhaps the Elizabethans, who could write equally freely on everything. [...]

To Tristan Jones
Stowe
11 Oct. 32

Do you want your pamphlets back at once? I haven't yet had time to look at them. For about the first time in my life I have too much to do: that is in working moderately hard for a scholarship, reading the *Kapital* – which I have read so much of per day, because it requires a good deal of effort to understand, and, till to-day, writing a paper on Auden for the Lit. Soc. at the rate of about 1,000 words to the hour .... So far I have found time to do everything except answer letters and take exercise. Ogden's *ABC of Psychology* is easily the best text-book I have yet come across – and all the psychology I know comes from that and from conversations with Joe and others. If I were you I should also start on the *Kapital* for economics – it's extremely worth while; very slow going, but not too difficult; at least I have found nothing I couldn't eventually understand in the first 400 pages. And it is a very great book, though he doesn't follow up half the really exciting ideas that his facts and theories might lead to.

Have you seen this month's *Adelphi*? J. M. Murry on the 'Religion of Marxism,' which apparently consists of obeying your strongest impulses! And Marxist Murry has just written a pamphlet on the *Fallacy of Economics*!

It seems to me that the I.L.P. is going to be a useful rubbish dump for all the Utopians and religious who might otherwise poison the Communists. That's where Laurence Whistler will go if you don't wake him up. Have you seen *Proletaria en avant*? He seems to be growing into the archetype of minor poet, obstinately refusing to make any contact with reality at all. For heaven's sake do something about him if you have the chance; every one who I know who knew him seems to have thought him worth while, but why must he write like that?

The pathetic pseudo-individualism of the English intelligentsia is what irritates me most. They won't turn Communist except with their own little reservations to explain why they are different from and superior to the orthodox Marxist. Even if they are in theory, that's not much help. I'd like to see how many workers have joined the Sexology Group, No. III. of the Promethean Society; or the Political Group associated with the Direct Action Group. It's rather pathetic at this time in particular.

Have you seen Auden's poem 'A Communist to Others,' in *Twentieth Century*? It isn't a good poem, but I think it's important, intelligible to every class in the country since about 1580. For the gap between the advanced poets and the public has been growing ever since then.

Can you tell me what the recent instructions of Comintern to the Communists here were? All I have found about it was a very biased paragraph in *The Times*, from which I couldn't gather the facts. The Book-room, 'we don't know why,' can't get the *Daily Worker*! Is there any Communist weekly paper that would do instead?

To Frances Cornford
[Stowe]
[Autumn 1932]

[…] John Strachey is admirable. He completely smashes Ortega y Gasset's thesis – shows that what O. calls the symptoms of mob rule are simply the symptoms of capitalist decline. He isn't, I think, a very original mind, but can apply the Marxist-Leninist thesis to the present situation extremely forcibly and convincingly. The difference in angle of the observer between him and Marx or Lenin is v. interesting – Marx and Lenin view history entirely from the angle of the industrial proletariat, Strachey selfconsciously views history from the angle of the capitalist and deals with all the capitalist economists in turn before he arrives at the Marxian interpretation.

You remember what you were telling me about the workers on the drive and Clare. This is what I mean by class-consciousness. Suppose the workman was able to say:

'I must live all my life in an over-crowded house and spend my day in long and heavy work for an unnecessarily low wage. At any moment, through no fault of my own, but simply because the capitalist class has failed (and must fail) to plan its production and distribution, I may be thrown out of work; in which case I shall rot alive, all my physical and mental powers slowly and inevitably decaying through inactivity. If I have any property, I must sell it and live on the proceeds before I can claim public assistance. I must spend my dotage either living on some relative who cannot afford to keep me, and must necessarily grudge me everything he gives me, or else I must go to the workhouse. And if I ever again find employment, I shall be forced down to subsistence level by wage-cuts, and there is no hope for myself or anyone in my class ever attaining to a fully developed, free and unanxious way of life. Moreover, this is not a catastrophe from heaven, that no one could prevent or foresee; it is due to the fundamental contradictions of the capitalist system; it has been prevented in Russia, it was foreseen by Marx.'

Then he would be what I should call class-conscious, and I should not blame him for hating the bourgeois class. At any rate, he might realise that their interests were essentially opposed – that they were enemies whether or not they hated. In fact, once he is class-conscious – and he must be, if he is to serve himself – to continue the present attitude wd., I think, be slightly servile.

From Frances Cornford
2 Dec. 32

[...] *I liked your eloquent speech of the workmen in the drive. I think that need be only the realisation of the appalling mess we are in & need not lead to class* hatred *& antagonism. If you and CFC both wanted to marry the same woman, it would be silly to pretend that you both could, or that one of you wouldn't suffer – but it would be the moment to avoid hatred, if any right settlement was to be arrived at, & to call up all the funds of goodwill, all your civilised instincts [I think it is a tragedy that classes & countries should have behaviour & standards expected of them that wouldn't be tolerated in an individual.], all the bonds you had in common.*

I think it is also a tragedy that Marx should be a Jew. The English may be racially mongrels but somehow their psyches are profoundly alike *I* know *– the difference between these men in the drive & me are superficial (even if one day, partly encouraged by you, they stone or shoot me) compared with our likeness. Our unconsciouses are much more alike than our consciouses – (that is why I think the English only split to remedy gross injustices & then cohere again.) But this is hard for any Jew to understand. One must always remember that the differences between them & the people of their adopted country are much more profound than they appear. The likeness is on the surface – they are profoundly different in their unconscious. So how can Marx be aware of the irrational likeness and solidarity of us English people, & how can he not simplify to a ludicrous point his rational opposition of capital & labour. And now he has left to every communist in this class-conscious business, a decent formula on which to hang all the basest passions of humanity – Patriotism was another such formula in the war – and I've lived through knowing what that was like.*

Well, well. Goodnight. It's hard to stop writing once one has begun.

From Frances Cornford
22 Primrose Hill Road, NW 3
Friday [Autumn 1932]

[…] You are quite right, that I was talking about why I didn't want communism. It must seem to you (perhaps quite rightly) like an already infected person talking about why they don't want measles – really futile – in fact & beside the mark – on the other hand, communist tactics seem to me sometimes like scratching from without till they have produced something resembling spots. And if measles aren't inevitable that's a definitely wicked thing to do to the body.

I am in a difficult position. I must feel *& know this thing for myself – and till I am stronger I have so little brains & time for reading, & a natural horror of the exaggeration & personal, heated bitterness of polemics, not sects. I don't think I feel any personal clinging onto privileges. It is always easier for anybody who has anything approaching the religious temperament to go the whole hog (that is why Middleton Murry is happy now) – to lay everything on an altar of a creative idea.*

But I haven't read enough to know intellectually the revolution must come & I don't feel *it – yet, that England wants it. I have felt things clearly sometimes about England that it didn't* want *war in 1914 & I think […] that it was ready for a generous settlement in 1918 – a thing that foreign Ll. G.* couldn't feel. But FMC felt this clearer, & I may have caught it from him.*

I wasn't a pacifist in 1914, & strangely enough I'm not ashamed. Because it was inevitable because I couldn't *have been anything else, then. But I am now. And you cannot I think be an honest pacifist & an honest revolutionary. So you will have to put up with me very indecisive and in bits, till something more happens to me. I am aware of something sentimental & untrue in this propaganda business. The Hunger Marchers ought to have been called Injustice Marchers. I doubt if any were* hungry. *Do you remember Helena describing a young man carrying along a girl in the crowd who had fainted. That's perhaps what you have to do in a Russian crowd – But in an English one you fall out & the police can quickly get an ambulance, or administer first aid – make the crowd give you*

air & so on. That was a tiny bit of theatricality. Was it symbolic?
1 think so. Also to refuse to let a deputation of themselves present
their petition. Alan Barlow* (& Esther) seemed quite clear they
were determined to be prevented presenting that petition. I enjoyed
talking to Alan, & I felt you would. Tho' I suppose he'd make you
gasp too much at his English amused tolerant limited idea-lessness.
But what of this remark 'Surely what's wrong with the world is
not any system, but human greed & shortsighted folly'? 'Ideas,' says
Alan, 'are all very well as long as they don't prevent you getting on
with the job.' 'What job Alan?' 'Why the job of keeping things going
of course'. Every obvious remark he makes is backed by his first-hand
experience – such as it is. 'When I was talking to the head of the
deputation of electrical engineers in the strike of so & so' – & so on.
The Barlows want to ask you for a weekend this holidays & I hope
you'll go – and suddenly get the supremely different point of view
of a typical someone who's trying to run the country – No, I think
he's only typically English, certainly all Civil Servants haven't
his firsthand honesty, though they may have his limitations. They
wouldn't like him give up travelling each day to town first class,
because he likes the people in the third class so much better.

But I'm getting garrulous. […]

To Frances Cornford
[Stowe]
[Autumn 1932]

I don't think of Communism as inevitable, like measles, or the
war, or the present crisis, but as *necessary*. It isn't an accident
that wd. come of its own accord from outside, even if no one
wanted it, like crisis, war, disease. But I think it's necessary; it
hasn't got to come; there's the alternative of gradually relapsing
into an American anarchy, as we are doing at present – also the
prospect of another war to 'save' the colonies. And I don't think
there's any demand for it in the people as a whole. There can be
no real demand for it till people become collectively conscious
of the difference industrialism has made and is making to their

lives. If they had been conscious of that all along they wd. have organised industry along socialist lines from the start, and so averted the crisis. But I think that to save themselves they have got to be made conscious. During the period of English industrial monopoly there was a steady rise of wages and growth of general prosperity; and not till they've realised that even if that state of affairs – England of '90–'14 – is desirable, it is absolutely unattainable, will they begin to look for a way out themselves. And there's a terrific organised conspiracy by the gutter press to persuade them to do nothing; the *Daily Mail* and the Beaverbrook press have been saying all this year that Crisis is over, and we shall soon have prosperity over again. And we've got to fight that, not just deplore it. It's only the middle generation and the pre-war trade unionists who know the period of English monopoly and believe they can return to it who are holding back a powerful revolutionary movement over here.

I think the Hunger Marchers really were hungry. I don't think it's a sentimentalism. B. Seebohm Rowntree calculates that the price of living for a family of 5 – *without considering rates or rents* – is 31s. 8d. I don't know how much a baby costs to feed – certainly it must be more than the 1s. it's allowed under the present Means Test; once rents and rates have been deducted, it might be possible to buy enough food for the week: but there is still the cost of lighting and fuel, as well as occasionally doctors, unemployment insurance, etc. In Stoke some families that had been evicted erected huts out of their furniture, and stretched sheets on top. They were *fined 10s.* and told that it wasn't allowed. And the iniquity of the Means Test is that, while formerly the dole was fixed, so that wages had to be a few shillings above, or else no one would work, the new provision is that benefit shd. be below the rate of wages – so that where one employer is able to enforce a wage-cut, the benefit-level in the whole district must come down. So I think they really were Hunger Marchers.

You're right that it's impossible to be a pacifist and a Communist. The Amsterdam Congress declared itself anti-pacifist. And I really don't see how any pacifist organisation wd. be strong enough to fight the Armament Firms, the Banks, and the Newspapers. It seems to me at present that Russia's the only country really out for disarmament – because it controls these things in its own country. I think revolution would be far less beastly than war; I quite see that in 1914 probably some sort of explosion was necessary; it needn't have taken the form it did – a business man's war. A revolution might have ended war for ever. 'The war to end wars' has simply made the technique of beastliness in war a great deal more efficient – the present govt., out for 'disarmament,' spends 125,000,000 on war, where in 1914 we only spent 78,000,000. True, the purchasing power of the £ has sunk, but now the price of munitions has fallen even further – so that we're preparing for war faster than in 1914. And exporting munitions to both China and Japan. The Labour Government hadn't the guts to fight the Armament firms and continued war preparations on the same scale, in spite of its sentimental pacifist propaganda. And that's all we've got out of the war to end wars. That's why I'm not a pacifist – however good the ideal, the absolute impossibility of attaining it without a fight.

To Tristan Jones
[Stowe]
[Autumn 1932]

Here they all are.* I only had time to read Cole's plan; but am sending them back because I don't suppose I ever shall have time. I was just a little disappointed with Cole's plan: I don't know enough economics to criticise it, for or against, but it seems sound. But I think it isn't a powerful enough emotional position to accumulate the colossal reserves of energy and fanaticism that are needed to bring through a revolution without violence; it seems to me too much a party programme like any other, without a sufficiently enthusiastic backing to bring it through. I think all the political creative activity of the country is going into the revolutionary parties. And I still don't understand the form his nationalisation is going to take; I think either we've got to set up workers' committees, which means Communism, so that we can go the whole way; or else the plan must have the capitalist and bourgeois consent. To control production it's obviously necessary to close down all the small concerns with obsolete machinery, whose production can't be made as paying as the large and well-equipped concerns. Therefore all these people have to be compulsorily closed down and compensated; compensation must come from profits; it must make up for the closed down works and yet not exceed the profits of those already engaged in production. So that the proportion of unpaid to paid labour must still remain very high.

And when technical improvements are introduced, so that productivity of labour is higher, and fewer workers are needed, either (a) workers are sacked, demand falls off, crisis again, or (b) if this isn't allowed, if the govt. forces the employers to invest in shorter hours, higher wages, etc., you get the situation of a govt. not truly representative of workers or capitalists, which yet must enforce its will on the capitalists without wholehearted workers' support. (On 2nd thoughts most of this argument doesn't at all apply to Cole; only to the theories of planned capitalism that Cole, I shd. think, would also oppose. Sorry. But it's helped me to get clear what I think.)

But I think Cole's Socialism is without the strength of Communism because it is without the really important part of Marxism, his dialectical materialism and the interpretation of history. Also I think he is over-confident about the extent of Russian co-operation; I think Russia wd. support the C.P. here against him. But nevertheless, it is a prodigious advance from anything of the L.P. that I've seen; I should hesitate to oppose them if I ever thought they were going seriously to attempt to carry through the entire programme. But I don't think they will. Not by 1936, anyway; there's too much readjustment inside the party to be done; and 1941 may be too late to prevent revolution, even if (unless the L.P. co-operates) too early for successful revolution. So I (largely for purely emotional reasons) would anyhow prefer to be in the C.P. though we might try and make it more sensible about men like Cole, who clearly are able and sincere. Also, of course, he has a big influence with the 'enlightened' bourgeoisie, though I don't think he has with the workers.

I don't think FCC* has yet made up her mind about Communism. Talking to me she'd be right; to a right person she'd be left. But it wd. always be a religious movement to her, and she'd never consider it from an intellectual standpoint – so that she won't ever take it up entirely. Also she makes objections that aren't at all relevant to the central problem; such as: some people are born to live in castles and some in cottages, some to command and some to serve, etc.: what matters is the inner spiritual freedom. Also the anti-Russian propaganda – the mass production of individuals, mechanisation of humanity. She has somehow confused Communism with mechanisation, though God knows that happens fast enough in capitalist countries. I think she'll come round part of the way; never the whole way. Nothing wd. make her revolutionary.

To Tristan Jones
[Stowe]
[Autumn 1932]

You misunderstand me. I don't say that Cole's position hadn't a wide enough emotional appeal; I said it wasn't a powerful enough emotional attitude. Of course I am as much against the Lib-Lab ILP emotional exploitation, the sentimental revolutionary anarchist sob-stuff of Emma Goldman, etc. – but that is the feeblest emotional attitude there is. But you'd agree that Lenin's (and even RPD's*) is a more powerful emotional position than Cole's – but is therefore less a popular 'emotional' – propagandist movement. By an emotional attitude I mean one which you can support in all your activities – as distinguished from the intellectual beliefs, say, that 2+2=4, or that joint stock banks must be nationalised. Cole's intellectual position obviously provides a complete emotional absorption and satisfaction for himself: but I don't think it's strong enough to carry much weight. It's too much a purely technical organisation. It hasn't the power of Marxist-Leninist dialectic, of being a complete philosophy of history and of evolution. Economically it is no more sound; its only advantage is its less violent method.

It seems to me an attempt to slur over the reality of the class struggle, by believing that most 'intelligent men and women' wd. support him. I think, even if he cd. come to power with that 'unpatriotic' programme in face of the banks, the armament makers and the gutter press, without revolution, he wd. have an organised counter-revolution to deal with – super sabotage that would *(a)* demand revolutionary measures to suppress and so destroy his one advantage over the C.P., *(b)* bring about a temporary material position v. close to starvation, as he himself says. And this will only be tolerated if it can have a powerful emotional position to support it – such as the Communist position in Russia, where the C.P. are quite deliberately responsible for a food shortage which cd. be avoided if they slowed down the plan to export less grain. They rightly won't, because they can still make use of the tremendous accumulation of energy that will tolerate the worsened conditions in the interests of the psychological success of the plan at full speed in spite of the need to export more grain, etc. Such an accumulation of revolutionary energy wd. be needed in England, both to defeat the bourgeois counter-attack and to last over the period of distress before Communism got going. Cole isn't strong enough to supply it.

It seems to me he is emasculating the real international force of the movement. His preface to *Das Kapital* immensely weakens his position, by his (as far as I can see) purely negative rejection of the Marxian Theory of Value. (For Cole, the only source of profit is co-operation; for Marx, not only co-operation, but the labour-time embodied in the surplus product.) As far as I can see he rejects the doctrine because of the practical difficulty (virtual impossibility) of applying it. But it's a purely ideal theory of value – there's no need to apply it to specific cases; the source of profit in them can be easily enough found from the individual items – wages, plant, raw materials, rent of buildings, etc. But the economic basis of capitalism depends on production for profit. Marx's theory explains the origin of profit better than any other. I see no reason to reject it unless a positively more applicable theory can be brought forward – Cole doesn't, I suppose, believe in Marshall's?

(Later. What I mean about the distinction between emotional and intellectual attitude. It's quite easy for any economics don to agree with Cole; he'll probably belong to SS LP* and vote Labour – like G. Shove at Cambridge. But, unless it is an emotional position too, he won't give up all his time and energy to it like Cole. This isn't a defence of emotional argument, or irrational sentimental Communism.) Apologies for incoherence of argument. [...]

Sorry my letters are so like manifestos.

*To Frances Cornford**
Boswells, Wendover
Bucks.
[1932/3]

[...] A very successful 4 days in London. Esther was busied with proofs, as the man who was to correct them with her has had to leave early and left too little time to finish then off. But she seemed well and extremely interesting as always. – I find that she agrees with me about 'The Waves', while John Sparrow, whom I met at the Keynes's* thinks it astonishingly good.

I met the Schiffs on Tuesday evening, and liked them better than ever. They both seem to be extremely generous about W. Lewis* – so much so that they seem really to enjoy the satire directed against them – SS says that its the best part of the book and advises me to read it as soon as I get hold of the copy. Mrs S. grew positively hilarious telling how W Lewis alleges that she has had her face lifted eighteen times.

Also the French pictures. I was very disappointed with Renoir, that Gwen and CFC enthuse so wildly about. He seemed to me entirely forceless and weak – but was tremendously impressed by the Cézanne: also by Toulouse-Lautrec, Gauguin and Daumier. Also, astonishingly good Millet and David, whom I had scarcely heard of before.

Also a smaller 20th century show at Leicester galleries, and was confirmed in my opinion of Picasso, whom I think very good indeed. I met an old clergyman there, who said he was a nephew of Frederick Walker, trying with a rather pathetic eagerness to understand the modern painters, but finding them very difficult and 'unlike Burne-Jones and Rossetti, on whom he had been brought up'.

*To Tristan Jones**
[London]
[Spring 1933]

Dear Tristan,

1 o'c. Nanking* Saturday? And afterwards come on to our study circle if you feel inclined.

At the moment I'm:

    Secretary FSS*

    Editor *Vanguard**

    Sec. L.R.D. Group*

    Sub-editor *Young Worker*

    L.S.E. Anti-Fascist Committee

    Marxist Society

    Anti-War Committee, etc.

So you see I haven't time to write.

To Frances Cornford
[Easter 1933]

[…] I got here after a most fantastic journey, through what should have been the worst part – the 3rd class from Toulon to Paris for 15 hours – I slept almost perfectly. Then for no apparent reason, as soon as I got onto the boat, I was sick for the rest of the way, although the sea was absolutely calm. What made it worse was that I had nothing to be sick with, as I'd had no breakfast. I must find out whether Ursula was likewise affected; my only explanation is that it was the curious vegetable we had eaten on the train the night before. However, I think Im absolutely recovered now.

I am glad about Jung. I think you should go to him as soon as you can. What I always feel about psychologists – at any rate looking through Adler's case-book (I dont know about Jung) – is that in general theyve only got the dregs of the unemployed rich to work on, who arent a representative cross-section of humanity, and who are mostly incurable from birth. Anyhow thats true of his European cases; I suppose the American rich have alive blood in them a much shorter while back. So from the point of view of psychology, the more real people with real problems who go, the better. And I am pretty certain that it would do you more good than anything else. I shouldnt wait till Clare goes to St. Georges. There's very likely to be a war or a revolution or both before then; if there isn't, you can go back again, if you want to, when she is there.

The S of F* was well worth it, though not perfectly successful. The place was a little below Margaret and Geoffrey's glowing descriptions; and there wasnt quite the right selection of people there, which was no ones fault. But I wished Joe had been able to come. I for one find it very difficult to be at ease in a hotel; and I think CFC found the same. But it was worth it for the sake of the sun and the sea and (sometimes) the hills.

You'll have got by now my polemic against Murry. Forgive my ignoring all the other points of your letter and addressing you like a public meeting; I was trying to get my own ideas straight as much as anything else. But I think there was sense in nearly all my points; Id like to talk it over with you & FMC. I cant quite grasp how your story from Catriona* relates to me, partly because I havent read the book. But if it means what I take it to mean, I think there's one slight confusion. You talk about the upset of a war as though it were a vague intangible thing that affected humanity in a sort of nebulous way and nothing else. But humanity is composed of individuals; and that upset means thousands of equally great injustices against individuals who are innocent, which offend the sense of justice just as much. But I cant really argue the point, because I didnt understand you well enough. Again Id like to talk that over.

To Tristan Jones
London
24 April 33

I've had to break with Elisabeth, and I should think for good. I'd seen it coming for some time back, but waited to see her to make certain. She can't lead the sort of life I do; and I neither can nor want to give it up. She's born in the wrong century; the fault for our failure isn't in ourselves so much as in the time we're living in. I tried to hope all the time that when she saw the real issues, not in terms of arguments round the fire, but among the workers, she'd feel that she'd have to come in. And I left France in a pretty inconclusive state. But when I saw the Y.C.L.* at the Young Worker Conference, I felt that the gap's too hopelessly wide. I am very sorry in one way, though I am always glad of any break with the past that reflects my own position from a new angle. If one's ready to kill and be killed for the revolution, this kind of break shouldn't make too much difference, Heil, Rot Front!

It would be interesting to see how long one would remain a Communist inside a Nazi barracks. That's the final test. I feel already I could stand any other. That one I don't know about.

To Frances Cornford
[London]
[Spring 1933]

[...] It may be I shall have to call off this weekend again as there's a strike situation developing in one of the tramway depots, so that I may be wanted down there. But I shall know definitely about that on Thursday. On the whole question of the relation of party work to anything else, if I am to explain the nature of the work I'm doing for the L.R.D. it might help you to understand my position. What happened was this: after I had collected the materials for my research work, the L.R.D. wrote round to the Trade Union Branches (not Co-operatives) saying that they had a speaker on the Transport Act who was prepared to speak at branch meetings. And since I've undertaken the job, when a branch applies for a speaker on a certain date, the L.R.D. clearly can't write back to say that their speaker is on holiday and can they hold a meeting some other time! because clearly the meetings are for the benefit of the audience and not the speaker, and obviously the branch must pick its own date. Since they can't always give very long notice, it's difficult for me to fix plans any time ahead. Although this is inconvenient it's completely counterbalanced by the significance of the job for me; it's far the most important job I've ever done in my life, or, most likely, will have for another three or four years. I'm tremendously lucky to have got this job, as it ought only to go to an experienced speaker and research worker, and I must make full use of it.

If you put yourself in my position you can see why I think it's so much more important now than anything else. I have to speak to a working-class audience, usually for the most part consisting of men twice my age, on a highly complicated technical subject. I'm almost without previous experience as a speaker or as a research worker. So you can see that it needs all the power I have to make a good job of it. From my own point of view you can see how urgently I want to bring it off. And the L.R.D., to which I am responsible as its representative, is in a very precarious position, and if I let the L.R.D. down, it weakens its support among the trade unionists – on whom it depends for its financial existence.

So far I've done as well as I could expect. The first meeting I undertook I was very nervous and also shaky on my material, and I was only saved from making a mess by the fact that I had a very sympathetic audience. Luckily I retrieved my failure as a speaker by making friends with the Secretary, who invited me to attend any branch meeting I liked, which is a big privilege for a non-unionist – almost like being admitted. The second time was much better than the first. The third time I was lucky enough to be at the top of my form; the branch secretary stood me a drink beforehand, with the result that I wasn't nervous before speaking! and spoke much better than I ever have anywhere before. You'll understand how tremendously it matters for me to keep this up, and why I must put it before anything else.

To ——
8 Jan. 36

[...] One good thing. An exhibition of Soviet Children's Art which was just terrific. Everything in *Inprecorr** about the joyous life and all that kind of thing is just true. It's just overflowing with life and incredibly good. The best bit of revolutionary propaganda for a long time.[...]

To ——
June, 1936

[...] I'll bring a copy of Peter's poems if I remember. A. L. Morton got the right line in the Daily *Worker* actually. The poems are too much: Look, I'm a Marxist, but even so I think flowers are beautiful and I can fall in love, etc., without being in any way false. But that seems really to me like for

Cézanne to say: 'Look, I'm an impressionist but I'll paint half my pictures pre-Raphaelite to show you I can.' What I mean is, to be revolutionary means to approach the whole reality there is, which is different and wider than other people's, in a different way. Not just to demonstrate that you are human, although that may be, as it were, a necessary foundation stage. [...]

I am beginning to feel more strongly than before about the theory of theory. The old concept of a working-class party was one of a small bunch of people who studied and converted people. The I.L.P.* used to make its reputation in Scotland because its speakers were people who could get up and explain to a bunch of bums how crises worked, or surplus value, and make it all interesting. And it was a colossal step forward when the C.P.G.B.* began to understand the need for having a line on everything. But we've carried it too far, have become too much empiricist and simple, and I am really alarmed about the number of people who are capable of putting the line clearly and simply, or explaining just why capitalism causes war if they're challenged, or even why the U.S.S.R. is any different, or all the simple things. The more you read about the Bolsheviks, the more it seems they *started* their contact with Marxist study circles and giving a really good training before passing on to the mass work: and that's why they had a party like they did. That's why I'm beginning to think that, for instance, the 20,000 people in the N.C.L.C.* are a thing of real importance for us to win.

To Frances Cornford
Conduit Head
[June 1936]

Thanks very much for your letter. I wasn't surprised by the first, but quite a lot by the distinction. It is really quite useful, as I now have £185 in scholarships for next year, and with one or two more odd jobs in teaching I hope to pick up will now be more or less self supporting: and its about time I was.

The thesis I want to work on is around the question of the social roots of the Elizabethan poets. The other night at supper I was explaining the lines of it to F.M.C. and was quite startled to find how much the general structure of my ideas had in common with his Thucydides. There are big differences of course, but I was surprised how much was the same. I'd like to show you the draft outline as soon as I can have it ready; that is if you feel up to it; but I think it might interest you and I'd certainly like to know what you thought.

Tomorrow I am going off to work for a bit on Justin's* farm. At the end of the exams, I was quite frightened the amount of muscle I'd lost in the last year or two. And before I open another book I want to do a bit of real hard physical work.
I'm sorry I don't write more often, but as you know I'm not so good at letters. [...]

Diary Letter to Margot Heinemann
[Aragon]
[16–30 August 1936]

Darling, I'll explain why in a minute, but just at the moment I'm spending whole days at the front with nothing to do, and so I am writing you an immense letter: if it wasn't so hot here I'd try and get my ideas and impressions sorted out, but I can't, so I'm writing everything down just as it comes out …. First of all, a last will and testament. As you know there is a risk of being killed. Statistically not very great, but it exists all the same. First of all, why I am here? You know the political reasons. There's a subjective one as well. From the age of seventeen I was in a kind of way tied down, and envied my contemporaries a good deal their freedom to bum about. And it was partly because I felt myself for the first time independent that I came out here. But I promise this is the last time I shall leave you unnecessarily. Maybe that the Party will send me, but after this I will always be with you when I have the chance. I love you with all my strength and all my will and my whole body. Loving you has been the most perfect experience, and in a way, the biggest achievement of my life.

The party was my only other love. Until I see you again, bless you my love, my strength. Be happy. I worked for the party with all my strength, and loved you as much as I was capable of. If I am killed, my life won't be wasted. But I'll be back.

Well, all that's said. At the moment I am on top of a hill at the front in Aragon. A complete circle of rocky mountains, covered with green scrub, very barren, with a few fields in between. Two kilometres away a village held by the enemy. A grey stone affair with a big church. The enemy are quite invisible. An occasional rifle shot. One burst of machine-gun fire. One or two aeroplanes. The sound of our guns sometimes a long way off. And nothing else but a sun so hot that I am almost ill, can eat very little, and scarcely work at all. Nothing at all to do. We lie around all day. At night two hours on the watch – last night very fine with the lightning flickering behind Saragossa, miles away. Sleeping in the open with a single blanket on the stones – last night it rained, but just not quite enough to get through the blanket. How long we are to be here I don't know. And now comes the catch – I came up to the front and Richard* was left behind. Enlisted here on the strength of my Party card. There was one little Italian comrade with some broken English. Now he's been sent off. So I'm here and the only communication I have is with the very broken French of a young Catalan volunteer. And so I am not only utterly lonely, but also feel a bit useless. However it couldn't have been expected that everything would go perfectly as it did to here. This loneliness, and this nervous anxiety from not knowing when or how to get back, and not yet having been under fire, means that inevitably I am pretty depressed. Even thought of using my press ticket to get home, but it would be too ridiculous to come out here to fight and go back because I was a bit lonely. So I am here provisionally until the fall of Saragossa whenever that is….

In the morning – it was a Sunday – before it was yet hot, the bells of the enemy village of Perdiguera sounded very slow and mournful across the distance. I don't know why, but that depressed me as much as anything ever has. However, I'm settling in now. Last night we began to make ourselves more comfortable – dug little trenches to sleep in and filled them with straw. So long as I am doing anything, however purposeless, I feel fine. It's inactivity that just eats at my nerves. But the night before last I had a dream. One of the toughest people when I was small at school was the captain of rugger, an oaf called D—— I was in the same dormitory and terrified of him. I hadn't thought of him for years, but last night I dreamt extremely vividly about having a fight with him and holding my own, and I think that's a good omen. I don't know how long we stay on this hill, but I am beginning to settle down to it…

Now a bit about the political situation. That isn't easy to get straight, particularly as I haven't yet heard anyone explain the position of the Party (and the militia here I am with are P.O.U.M. – left sectarian semi-Trotskyists). But roughly this. The popular front tactics were worked magnificently to begin with. They won the elections. And under the slogan of defence of the Republic, they enabled us to arm the workers when the Fascist revolt started. Up till then the position is quite clear. But now in Catalonia things are like this. There is a left Republican Government. But, in fact, the real power is with the workers. There are 50,000 or more armed workers in Catalonia – and in the Barcelona patrols they are organised in the following proportions: 325 C.N.T.* (Anarchist), 185 E.R.C.* (left Republican), but this means simply the Civil Guard and the Guardia de Asalto, the police; 145 U.G.T.* (Soc.-Com.); 45 P.O.U.M. Thus the Anarchists predominate. Seventy-five per cent. of industry is already socialised – and mostly worked by the Anarchists. In order to prevent a Fascist outbreak, every night splits, unpopular bosses, and known Fascists are taken for a ride. Assisted by the militia, there is a peasant war raging in the countryside and thousands of Kulaks and landlords have been killed. The Anarchists appear to be preparing to attack the Government after the fall of Saragossa. That would be disastrous. The only possible tactics for the Party are to place themselves at the head of the movement, get it under control, force recognition from the Government of the social gains of the revolution, and prevent at all costs an attack on the Government – unless the Government actually begin to sabotage the fight against Fascism. That may be what the Party is doing. But I have a fear that it is a little too mechanical in its application of People's Front tactics. It is still concentrating too much on trying to neutralise the petty bourgeoisie – when by far the most urgent task is to win the anarchist workers, which is a special technique and very different from broad Seventh Congress phrases. But I don't really know....

In Barcelona one can understand physically what the dictatorship of the proletariat means. All the Fascist press has been taken over. The real rule is in the hands of the militia committees. There is a real terror against the Fascists. But that doesn't alter the fact that the place is free – and conscious all the time of its freedom. Everywhere in the streets are armed workers and militiamen, and sitting in the cafés which used to belong to the bourgeoisie. The huge Hotel Colon overlooking the main square is occupied by the United Socialist Party of Catalonia. Further down, in a huge block opposite the Bank of Spain, is the Anarchist headquarters. The palace of a marquis in the Rambla is a C.P. headquarters. But one does not feel the tension. The mass of the people are oblivious of the Anarchist-Government trouble brewing, and simply are enjoying their freedom. The streets are crowded all day, and there are big crowds round the radio palaces. But there is nothing at all like tension or hysteria. It's as if in London the armed workers were dominating the streets – it's obvious that they wouldn't tolerate Mosley or people selling Action in the streets. And that wouldn't mean that the town wasn't free in the real sense. It is genuinely a dictatorship of the majority, supported by the overwhelming majority. Not yet in Soviet form – the elections to the committees aren't on the basis of localities or factories but representatives of organisations. That narrows the basis a bit, but not much, as a huge majority of the people are organised.

Going into action. Thank God for something to do at last. I shall fight like a Communist if not like a soldier. All my love. Salute.   JOHN

Up till now this letter has been miserable. For this reason. I came out with the intention of staying a few days, firing a few shots, and then coming home. Sounded fine, but you just can't do things like that. You can't play at civil war, or fight with a reservation you don't mean to get killed. It didn't take long to realise that either I was here in earnest or else I'd better clear out. I tried to avoid the dilemma. Then I felt so lonely and bad I tried to get a pass back to Barcelona. But the question was decided for me. Having joined, I am in whether I like it or not. And I like it. Yesterday we went out to attack, and the prospect of action was terribly exhilarating – hence the message on the top of the page. But in the end we went back without doing anything. But I am settling down, picking up scraps of the language and beginning to feel happy. I think I'll make a good fighter, and I'm glad to be here. And since they won't let me go, it means that I don't feel useless or in the way, as if I were I'd be sent back. So I'll probably be here two months, and I will learn a hell of a lot. There is a 70 per cent. chance of getting back uninjured and 90 per cent. of getting back alive; which is, on the whole, worth while – and even if it wasn't, I'd have to stay.

Altogether I've passed the worst days of mental crisis, though all the physical hardship is to come. But I think I'll bear up. I've got a kind of feeling, rather difficult to explain, that my personality, I myself, was beginning to assert itself again. For days I've been shoved about from place to place, lost and anxious and frightened, and all that distinguished me personally from a unit in the mass obliterated – just a unit, alternately worried, home-sick, anxious, calm, hungry, sleepy, uncomfortable in turn – and all my own individuality, such strength as I have, such ability to analyse things, submerged. Now that's beginning to be different, I am beginning to adapt. Probably I'll be swept off my feet again when the first action starts. But now I, John Cornford, am beginning to emerge above the surface again and recognise myself and enjoy myself, and it feels good.

The army is a curious mixture of amateur and professional. There is practically no shouting and saluting. When somebody is told to do something, he gets up to do it all right, but not in a hurry. Officers are elected by acclamation, and obeyed. About half the troops are more or less in uniform, in blue or brown overalls and blue shorts. The rest are more or less nondescript. I myself am wearing a pair of heavy, black, corduroy trousers (expropriated from the bourgeoisie), a blue sports shirt, and that alpaca coat, rope-soled sandals, and an infinitely battered old sombrero. Luggage, a blanket, a cartridge case (held together with string) in which there is room for a spare shirt, a knife, tooth-brush, bit of soap, and comb. Also a big tin mug stuck in my belt. But most are a good bit smarter than that.

What is new is the complete feeling of insecurity, new for me, but most workers have it from the day they leave school. Always in all my work before there has been the background of a secure and well-provided home, and friends that I could fall back upon in an emergency. Now that is no longer here, I stand completely on my own. And I find that rather difficult at first. But I shall manage. Just now, for instance, I have unlimited opportunity to write. And I have plenty of things which for years I've wanted to write. But I can't get them together in my head, things aren't straight enough: all I can put down are my immediate subjective impressions, and I can't think about Birmingham or anywhere else. Oh, for the objectivity of Nehru. I'll learn: I am learning. But it's going to be something of a testing-time.

Yesterday I watched from the tiled roof of our hut the aerial bombardment of Perdiguera. The planes circling slowly and high above; then you would see a huge cloud of dust rising, beginning to float away, and then, seconds later, the sound of the crash. The comrades with me on the roof were shouting for delight as each bomb landed. I tried to think of the thing in terms of flesh and blood and the horror of that village, but

I also was delighted. Now as I write three enemy planes have passed by and out of sight, but you can hear the thud of their bombs somewhere behind our lines.

Yesterday for the first time I was under fire. This is how it all happened, and it is one of the most curious experiences of my life. I found in the evening that we were due to make a surprise attack. That same evening there had arrived at Llecinena (Lerida) a new group of Italians. We lit a fire in the backyard, and I was given a chicken to pluck. Then the leader of the group, who for days now has let the house get into an indescribably filthy mess, suddenly set to work to straighten everything out and prepared a most extraordinary meal, the first we have had with clean cutlery and a clean table-cloth. After we had finished and smoked a cigarette – by now I am getting very used to listening to conversations of which I don't understand a word – we got our things together and marched out! We were kept waiting for an hour or two in the square, and I twice fell asleep on the pavement – for that morning I had decided that so little was happening and we were getting so much sleep at night, I wouldn't sleep any more during the day. Then after a bit we marched off. Halted on the road and again fell asleep. Even then the indiscipline of our troops struck me. Every one was whispering, and then every one would suddenly start shushing and altogether there was quite a noise. I was feeling quite good and cheerful then. After a bit we left the road, which was soft under foot and powdery with dust, and turned off into the mountains. We marched all night through the mountains, across the little, banked-up strips of field they have in Aragon, through stubble. For a while I slipped and floundered, then more or less fell into the rhythm. Then gradually it began to get light and I realised that this wasn't a night attack at all. Then far below us on the right we saw the lights of Saragossa. After that we halted for a bit, and a comrade pointed out to me Perdiguera miles below. I had no idea we had climbed so high. Then at last I understood the manoeuvre. By a night's march through the mountains we had got completely in the rear of the enemy. Sebastian, the fat

Rumanian, who was more exhausted than anyone else by the climb, began to try and sing a song from the *Meistersingers*, but I couldn't make out the tune. Then we went down. We were sorted out into groups, but almost immediately were dissolved again in the confusion. From on top of a hill – it was now about 5–6, and full day – we could see Perdiguera. Then we went down again and there was a ridge which hid it from view. Then the advance began. Our single column spread out like a fan over the parched earth of the fields, and we began to move quickly. I threw away the blanket I had carried all night for it was already hot. Then we came over the ridge in sight of the enemy, and at the same time heard an attack open up on the other side of the village. We moved forwards and were soon crouching in the vineyards a few hundred yards from the village, and for the first time heard shots whistling overhead. It was then our total lack of discipline made itself felt. The houses of the village came quite close on the left, but on the right were hidden by a ridge and only the church tower showed. But it seemed clear to me that we should attack to the right, because there was the enemy machine-gun which was holding up our counter-attack. But no such thing. A group of us crossed the fields in front of the vineyards and crossed with good cover below an olive field, the last stretch before reaching the village. Another group dashed off to attack the houses on the left and managed to get right up to them. All this time I hadn't the faintest idea who was winning or losing. Then I began to understand the planless nature of the attack. The group I was with was recalled back to the vines. There I began to collect the completely unripe grapes in my hands and suck the juice out of them. It didn't do much to relieve thirst, but it left a clean acid taste in the mouth. Then I saw the group which had taken the houses on the left come pouring back and take shelter. All this time I had not felt the least nervousness, but that may be because so far no one had been hit. I was surprised that the kick of my mauser was so slight – I hadn't had a chance of using it before – but all the same I couldn't get it under control. All this time I couldn't see any of the enemy, and so confined myself to shooting at doors and windows. Then quite suddenly we heard the noise of enemy planes. We crouched quite still among the vines: I was together with a lone Italian, Milano, a member of my group, and did what he did. Apparently the planes didn't notice us. They confined themselves to bombing the other side of Perdiguera, where we were attacking. But after the bombardment our forces were completely dispersed – not out of cowardice, no one was in the least frightened, but simply through lack of leadership, no one had said where to go and all had taken cover in different directions. So Milano decided to retreat, and I followed him. A group of about fourteen collected, and we marched back. Presently we came to a well – a big, open, stone affair about six yards across. On top was floating a dead rat. We stopped for a drink, though Milano said we might be captured because of it. Then, as we were going back, we saw a group of men in the vines and marched back to them. But there weren't many there. I went to sleep for a few minutes in the vines, but was soon woken up and told we should retreat. We retreated to a big stone barn on a slope above the well. Resting, in the barn a discussion was held. At last one comrade, a strong and intelligent-looking worker in overalls, took the initiative and introduced some kind of order. I couldn't understand the discussion, but I made out that a committee of three was being elected to take a decision on what to do. And in the end it was decided to retreat. On the way down I borrowed a mug off a comrade to go down to the well for a drink. I had a drink and several others followed. (We had been about twenty-five in all in the barn.) Then suddenly bullets began to whistle very close – zip – zip – zip. We crouched under the shadow of the stone rim of the well. Then eventually we sprinted up the fields in short bouts, bent double with the bullets all around us. After that we could retreat in peace. We marched back across the fields to the hills. My throat was utterly dry, so thirsty I could not swallow, and hungry and very weary. It was only by a desperate physical effort of the guts that I was able to move one foot after the other. The climb up the mountains was a serious affair because the heat of the sun was colossal. I placed myself behind Milano, who was a mountaineer, and followed as closely as I could the deliberate economy of his footsteps. We reached the top, and in spite of the fiasco I was beginning to feel better. At least I felt equal to the others, when, before, I had felt rather like a sham soldier. And this was exactly the kind of physical endurance my body was best capable of producing – certainly I was no more weary than the others and certainly made less fuss about water. The group split into two halves, one going off after water, the other with Milano keeping up high. Nearing the top the breeze was a real relief, and we came into a pinewood, the first proper vegetation for days. Then as we came out of the wood we saw some sheds below on the right. We went down to look for water. There was a well and a lame old man sitting by it. We hoisted the water in a leaky bucket. Just to show how thirsty I was, though the bucket was leaking rapidly I was able to fill and empty the cup (2/3 pint) five times before the bucket was empty. I noticed that the more experienced drank less. Then we went off to the barn and slept for three hours. Afterwards the old man put us on to a road, we moved slowly down, at his cripple's pace, through cypress woods, past those barren strips of climbing fields, past great slabs of marble sticking out of the hills, stopping at every well to drink. The worst was over. The rest was down hill. When we reached the first outpost we learned that five men had been killed in the frontal attack that day. Then home, past the big amphitheatre round the stagnant village pond with its green reeds, past the bare strip of earth which was a football ground, and back into Llecinena.

One thing that will come out of this. After having seen all the mistakes in organisation, all the inefficiency, and yet the revolution is winning, I think I shall have far more confidence in my own organising ability in such a situation. There are a whole lot of things I think I could do if I understood the language. And in spite of the fact that I understand so little, I think it will be possible to learn a good deal of military stuff – though the conditions here are so unique that there will probably be no opportunity of applying it – unless in Saragossa it is a question of street fighting.

The luckiest accident of the whole war was that which put me in touch with the German comrades. From this time on the days, which had dragged and stuck and jammed like a cart in a wet road, began to rotate slowly and regularly like the wheels of a train just gathering steam. I think the days spent in the village alone were the hardest I have yet spent in my whole life. It was the same loneliness and isolation as the first term in a new school, without the language and without any kind of distraction of something to do. All the revolutionary enthusiasm was bled out of me. I simply counted the hours. But the Germans are a splendid lot – and incidentally have treated me with a quite extraordinary personal kindness; and at last I can live in the present, get outside of my own mind, and carry on until it is time to go back.

I was never more glad of anything in my life than the accident which threw me together with them. Four of them are ex-members of the party; one still a member. They have left because they genuinely believe the C.I.* has deserted the revolution. Partly, perhaps, it is the uprootedness of emigrants. I do not know enough of the Spanish position to argue with them successfully. But I am beginning to find out how much the Party and the International have become flesh and blood of me. Even when I can put forward no rational argument, I feel that to cut adrift from the Party is the beginning of political suicide.

By far the greatest need is for something to read. In this heat, in spite of the fact that for two days we've been doing nothing in the shade of the monastery, it's very hard to sit down and study a language. I've forced myself to do about an hour and a half's German to-day, but only by an effort. About all one can do under these conditions is read. It isn't easy to write anything coherent or sensible.

To-day I found with interest but not surprise the distortions in the P.O.U.M. press. The fiasco of the attack on Perdiguera is presented as a punitive expedition which was a success.

Again into action for the attack on Huesca ... So far there has been no fighting in this advance, and only under an inaccurate rifle fire for a few minutes. And I am now rested and fed, and feeling happy and content. All I want is some English cigarettes, some English tea, strong (insular, but can't be helped).

Since meeting the Germans I feel like myself again, no longer lost, and revolutionary again. Before I was too lost to feel anything but lost. Now I'll fight like hell and I think I'll enjoy it. They are the finest people in some ways I've ever met. In a way they have lost everything, have been through enough to break most people, and remain strong and cheerful and humorous. If anything is revolutionary it is these comrades.

To F. M. Cornford
Toulouse Gare
Tuesday 5 a.m. [15 or 16 Sept. 36]

I've written to you several times from Spain, but I'm rather afraid, because I've had no replies, that nothing has been getting through. So I'm afraid you may have been anxious about where I am. After I left you in Cambridge the idea suddenly occurred to me to go to Spain for a few days: I expected at that time that the fighting would be over very soon: so in a tremendous hurry I got a letter of introduction from the News Chronicle and set out. After I had been three days in Barcelona it was clear, first, how serious the position was; second, that a journalist without a word of Spanish was just useless. I decided to join the militia: and I wrote you at once, but I'm terribly afraid that owing to censorship troubles nothing in English or German from the front has got through. I haven't yet been discharged from the militia, but have been sent back for a period of three weeks on a special propaganda mission; but I'll be able to talk over the whole position with you as soon as I am back. Had a fairly quiet month at the Saragossa and Huesca fronts, actively did only a little skirmishing; passively, was bombarded a bit, but only with fairly light artillery and air raid bombs. On that sector it is more an endurance test than anything else.

I hope you haven't been too much worried about me. Give my love to Hugh and Clare, if they aren't yet back at school. I hope it's been a good holiday.

To His College Tutor
4 Oct. 36

I am writing this letter to resign my scholarships, as by the time this reaches you I shall already be on the way to rejoin the unit of the Anti-Fascist Militia with which I have been fighting this summer. I am sorry I did not have time to discuss it personally. I should like to take this opportunity of thanking you, and through you other Fellows of the College I have not had time to write to, for the tremendous personal kindness and interest you have always shown me, even though you must have looked with disfavour on many of my activities.

To Margot Heinemann
[Spain]
[Autumn 1936]

Darling – I don't know whether you've got any of my letters; but as things stand I am getting on well enough. Being trained up, having a fairly good time well fed & the best drinks in the world, thinking of nothing but food & drink & smokes & fatigues & things like that. With a very good gang. Nearly all the English good, some of them very good: & the others some of them really first class. There isn't anything very much I can say. It is a good country here: and I'm quite enjoying things. But there's very little apart from that to say. I'll probably be here for a very long time. I don't think this war will be over for a long time, but I am more certain than ever that we're going to win. It's a matter of several days yet before going to the front.

And meanwhile an interesting life; very little responsibility, not knowing what's going to happen next, simply doing what we're told, not learning enough, but learning a good deal all the same. *[censored]*

To Margot Heinemann
[Spain]
[Autumn 1936]

My dearest – Things haven't been going so badly since my last letter. We are forming part of the big 5th Regiment, an International column, mostly refugees or foreign workers living in France, a really tough crowd, militarily trained, and a real lot of really good guys. Organization good: discipline not perfect but far better than any Spanish unit I have yet seen. Altogether so far I'm well pleased: it makes a hell of a difference to be fighting with people you can be proud of as a unit & who are enthusiasts for the same politics as yourself. At the moment we're doing very little but drilling: which wd. be useless in open country from a military point of view, but good in getting almost mechanically a bunch of sous-officiers with some confidence and responsibility – & the lack of them means a big problem still in the Spanish army.

Politically things seem fine. This district & all the way to Alicante is dominated by the party. The Anarchists are enthusiastically saluting U.S.S.R. which they called a slave state when I left Spain last. Viva Russia is the most popular slogan here. A good many discomforts: 3 shithouses for 700 men, & so filthy one has to fix a gas mask arrangement. But apart from the quite big dangers of disease (Bernard was taken off yesterday with a temperature of 103) we get on well enough.

The impressive thing about the towns is the complete economic stability. No panic. The p's in complete possession of the small businesses but neither hoarding nor sticking up prices; everywhere confidence in victory, the same as in Barcelona. I can't judge the arms situation, but at least it isn't desperate.

There's no doubt whatever in my mind we're going to win the war. I reckon 6–9 months as the probable duration. Went to a bull fight this afternoon. Only novices, & it was dull, bloody, & unaesthetic, the crowd clapping everything it could but more of the time giving the raspberry. One sees how good it could be, though.

It will probably be a matter of weeks before I get to the front, & then a short life but a merry one. Anyhow, I can fight with all my force with this bunch, which I couldn't with P.O.U.M.

To Margot Heinemann
[Spain]
21 Nov. [36]

It's a long time since I've written, but I simply haven't had the chance, as the last ten days we've been at the front just by Madrid, in the open all day. This is real war, not a military holiday like the Catalan affair. We haven't done any fighting yet: we are a group with a French machine-gun company which has been in reserve most of the time. I'm writing in the sunlight in a valley full of oaks, with one section leader twenty yards away explaining the Lewis gun to a group of French. But though we haven't yet fought, we've been having a sample of what's to come this winter. Three times heavily and accurately bombarded by artillery – and there are first-class German and Italian gunners.

But the main trouble is the cold. It freezes every night, and we sleep in the open sometimes without blankets. The trouble is that the offensive on Madrid became so hot that we were called out before our training was over, and without proper equipment. But our International Brigade has done well. Continuous fighting, heavy losses, many of them simply due to inexperience, but we've been on the whole successful.

The Fascist advance guard got very close to Madrid: but as I've always said, their main trouble is shortage of men, and they can't make a concerted advance: they push forward in alternate sectors. And we've given the head of their advance a hell of a hammering.

I don't know what the press is saying over in England: but Madrid won't fall: if we get time to organise and to learn our guns, we shall do very well.

Now as to our personnel. Less good news. Our four best Lewis gunners were sent up with an infantry section. One is in hospital with two bullets in the guts. Steve Yates (ex-corporal in the British army, expelled and imprisoned for incitement to mutiny) is missing, believed 90 per cent. certain dead. Worst of all, Maclaurin, picked up dead on his gun after covering a retreat. He did really well. Continuously cheerful, however uncomfortable, and here that matters a hell of a lot. Well, it's useless to say how sorry we are; nothing can bring him back now. But if you meet any of his pals, tell them (and I wouldn't say it if it weren't true) he did well here, and died bloody well.

Then worse still, our section leader, Fred Jones, he was a tough, bourgeois family, expelled from Dulwich, worked in South American Oil. Has been three years in the Guards, a hell of a good soldier, unemployed organiser, etc. Did magnificently here. Kept his head in a tough time after our captain got killed, and was promoted to section leader. Then on a night march got caught in some loose wire when a lorry passed, hurled over a bridge, and killed. We didn't see what happened: and to give some idea of the way we felt about him, after his death none dared to tell the English section for several hours. Well, we shall get along somehow. But that's a hell of a way to have your best man killed.

Bernard* has been doing fine. Worked terribly hard as liaison man and political delegate because of his knowledge of French: and he hasn't much reserve of physical strength. Two nights running he fainted from the cold, but hasn't made any complaints. There's a tough time ahead, and those that get through will be a hell of a lot older. But by Christ they'll learn a lot.

There's little enough else to say. Everyone here is very tired by the cold nights, often sleepless, a bit shaken and upset by our losses, depressed. And it's affected me a bit, though I'm getting a thick skin. If I'd written a few hours ago you'd have got a different kind of letter. For five weeks I scarcely missed you, everything was so new and different, and I couldn't write but formal letters. Now I'm beginning to wake up a bit, and I'm glad as I could be that the last few days I had with you were as good as they could be. I re-read your letter to me yesterday, and I was proud as hell. And as you say there, the worst won't be too hard to stand now. I don't know what's going to happen, but I do know we're in for a tough time. And I am glad that you are behind me, glad and proud. The losses here are heavy, but there's still a big chance of getting back alive, a big majority chance. And if I didn't, we can't help that. Be happy, darling. Things here aren't easy, but I never expected them to be. And we'll get through them somehow, and I'll see you again, bless you, darling.   JOHN

    – I felt very depressed when I wrote this. Now I've eaten and am for the moment in a building. I feel fine. Warm. I'll get back to you, love, don't worry. God bless you.

To Margot Heinemann
[Spain]
8 Dec. 36

Darling, There is an English comrade going back, and this is my first chance of an uncensored letter. Remember that a good deal is not for publication. Excuse incoherence, because I'm in hospital with a slight wound and very weak. I'll tell you about that later.

    I'll assume none of my letters have yet got through, as I've had no answers. First of all about myself. I'm with a small English group in the Machine Gun Company of the French Battalion of the First International Brigade. Luckily we are in the best company, the machine gunners; and in the best section of that, a Franco-Belgian section.

    Now, as to the English blokes. Amongst the good blokes,

Bernard, who is political delegate, replacing me because I did not speak enough French to get things done. He's been ill, and suffers terribly from the cold, but has borne up really well. John Sommerfield, tough and starting like me with no military training, has become a good soldier, and a good scrounger which is very important in a badly equipped army. David Mackenzie, a Scots student: age 19: first-class rifle shot and machine gunner: intellectual and writes good verse. A very good guy is Edward Burke of the *Daily Worker.* Ex-actor, looks like a sap, always loses everything, but has a queer gift for understanding machinery, became a good machine gunner in no time, was put *pro tem* on a trench gun, promoted to section leader he did well on a really nasty bit of the front line.

We had about a month's training at Albacete and La Rada. We English did badly, we were a national minority very hard to assimilate, mucked about between one station and another, starting work on one kind of gun and then having it taken away from us, taking part in manoeuvres which those that didn't speak French couldn't understand. When we at last got down to work with the machine gunners our training was interrupted almost before we started, and we were switched through to the front. That was early in November. We were put in general reserve in the University City, thought we could rest and take it easy. The first morning we were heavily shelled with 75's. I did quite well that day. The section leader, Fred Jones, was away, and so confident that all was quiet that he hadn't appointed a successor. I took charge on the moment, was able to get all the guns – we then had four – into position, and rescued one which the gunmen had deserted in a panic. But there was no attack after all.

Then in reserve in the Casa del Campo: a big wood, ex-royal forest, rather Sussexy to look at: but behind to the right a range of the Guadarama, a real good range with snow against a very blue sky. Then a piece of real bad luck. Maclaurin and three other Lewis gunners were sent up to the front. The French infantry company they were with was surprised by the Moors. The Lewis gunners stayed to cover the retreat. Mac was found dead at his gun, Steve Yates, one of our corporals, an ex-soldier and a good bloke, was killed too. Another, wounded in the guts. It's always the best seem to get the worst.

Then for the first time up to the front. We advanced into position at exactly the wrong time, at sunset, taking over some abandoned trenches. The Fascists had the range exact and shelled us accurately. Seven were killed in a few minutes. We had a nasty night in the trenches. Then back into reserve. The main trouble now was the intense cold: and we were sleeping out without blankets, which we had left behind in order to carry more machine-gun ammunition. Worse still to come; we had to make a night march back. There was a lorry load of wounded behind us. The lorry driver signalled, but wasn't noticed and got no answer. The four lines were so indeterminate that he thought we were a Fascist column and accelerated past us. Someone put up a wire to stop the car. The wire was swept aside, caught Fred Jones by the neck, hauled him over the parapet and killed him. Fred was a really good section leader: declassed bourgeois, ex-guardsman unemployed organiser, combination of adventurer and sincere Communist: but a really powerful person and could make his group work in a disciplined way in an army where there wasn't much discipline. That day the French redeemed their bad start by a really good bayonet attack which recaptured the philosophy building. We were in reserve for all this.

Then a spell of rest behind the lines. Back at the front in a really comfortable position in the philosophy and letters building. This was our best front line period. Comfortable, above all warm, and supplies regular. A great gutted building, with broken glass all over, and the fighting consisted of firing from behind barricades of philosophy books at the Fascists in a village below and in the Casa Velasques opposite. One day an anti-aircraft shell fell right into the room we were in. We were lucky as hell not to be wiped out completely: as it was there were only three slightly wounded, I gathering a small cut in the head. After the night in the rather inefficient but very nice Secours Rouge Hospital, where the amateur nurses wash your wounds like scrubbing the floor, I came back, feeling all right, but must have been a bit weak from loss of blood. Then came two heavy days work trench-digging in the frozen clay. The afternoon of the second day I think I killed a Fascist. Fifteen or sixteen of them were running from a bombardment. I and two Frenchmen were firing from our barricades with sights at 900: We got one, and both said it was I that hit him, though I couldn't be sure. If it is true, it's a fluke, and I'm not likely to do as good a shot as that again. Then back again into reserve. The first day we were there, David Mackenzie and I took a long walk towards the Guadarama. When I came back my wound began to hurt again: this morning I was very weak, a kind of retarded shock, I think, and am now in hospital for the time being.

Well, that's how far we've got. No wars are nice, and even a revolutionary war is ugly enough. But I'm becoming a good soldier, longish endurance and a capacity for living in the present and enjoying all that can be enjoyed. There's a tough time ahead but I've plenty of strength left for it.

Well, one day the war will end – I'd give it till June or July, and then if I'm alive I'm coming back to you. I think about you often, but there's nothing I can do but say again, be happy, darling. And I'll see you again one day.

Bless you,

JOHN

AFTERWORDS

Afterword
by Richard Baxell

2016 marks eighty years since the brilliant young student John Cornford was killed fighting for the Spanish Republican government in its desperate struggle to defeat the rising launched by the military and supported by most of the Right. It is also forty years since this collection of Cornford's writings was first published and nearly thirty years since the most recent edition.

Despite the passing of the years, the role of Cornford and his comrades in the International Brigades, and the civil war itself, remains a live issue in Spain and still provokes bitter division. Groups such as A.A.B.I., the *Asociación de amigos de las brigadas internacionales*, express their gratitude towards the international volunteers by campaigning to erect monuments and by holding commemorations. The Socialist Party (the P.S.O.E., which was part of the Republican coalition government during the civil war) provides support from within the parliament, which led to José Luis Zapatero's government passing the Law of Historical Memory in 2007; this included a clause awarding Spanish nationality to survivors of the International Brigades. However, Mariano Rajoy's *Partido Popular* (with its roots in *Alianza Popular*, founded by the Francoist minister, Manuel Fraga), has recently curtailed state help for the exhumation of Franco's victims, arguing that Spaniards need to forget the war and must not reopen old wounds. Meanwhile numerous memorials in honour of the International Brigades across Spain have been attacked and defaced.

There is less hostility in Britain, where veterans of the International Brigades have long been admired.[1] Yet here, too, they have their detractors. For many years, cold-war *realpolitik*

---

1   See, for example, 'Last of the Brigade', *The Guardian*, 10 November 2000.

saw the western democracies' lauding of Franco as a bulwark against communism. Alongside this, an interpretation that is deeply sympathetic to the anti-Stalinist P.O.U.M. and Anarchists (owing much to George Orwell's 1938 memoir *Homage to Catalonia* and, more recently, Ken Loach's film *Land and Freedom*) has seen the Communist-dominated International Brigades portrayed in a negative light. Sadly, the sacrifices made by Cornford and the other thirty-five thousand volunteers from around the world have not always been as appreciated as perhaps they should.

Yet within most histories of the British volunteers in Spain, the name John Cornford has had great significance. He was the subject of a memorial volume compiled by Pat Sloane in 1938, and of a meticulous joint biography by Peter Stansky and William Abrahams in 1966. Most recently, George Galloway paid him tribute as part of BBC Radio Four's *Great Lives* in September 2009. Young, good-looking, privileged, intellectual, erudite and political, Cornford epitomises popular notions of a young volunteer in Spain, his head swathed in bandages, scribing poetry as shells explode all around him. However, the Cambridge-educated great-grandson of Charles Darwin, son of a classical scholar and poet, was utterly unrepresentative of the vast majority of the overwhelmingly proletarian International Brigades. His comrades were fully aware of his outstanding qualities, noting his 'great brain' and powerful charisma; one later described him as 'like a bloody Greek god'.[2] Cornford, however, was accepted as well as respected by his comrades, with a reputation for fearless bravery and unselfishness under fire.

As Jonathan Galassi points out in his introduction to this edition, had John Cornford not died at such a young age – he had just turned twenty-one when he was killed – it is hard to imagine that he would not have gone on to have a brilliant career. This might have been in any number of arenas: while conventionally described as 'the poet John Cornford', he was by

2 Interview with Chris Thornycroft, Imperial War Museum Sound Archive interview 12932, reel 1, and with Sidney Quinn, interview 801, reel 1.

no means only a poet. Certainly his fiancée Margot Heinemann never felt comfortable with him being described as such and states that Cornford considered himself to be an active communist and full-time revolutionary rather than a poet.[3] He was certainly no naive idealist. The letters in this collection show clearly that though he was always a devout believer in the Republic's cause, he was candid and realistic about his time in Spain. His account of his time on the front line suggests not so much surging enthusiasm and adventure, but loneliness and homesickness. As he explained in a letter to Margot, this was 'a real war, not a military holiday'.[4] Unfortunately real wars entail real casualties; like many others whose lives were cut short in Spain (and the world war that followed), Cornford 'showed a promise that the fate of battle did not allow to be fulfilled'.[5]

Cornford's loss was keenly felt, not just by his comrades in Spain, but in Cambridge, where he had already established himself as a sincere young man, with an enviable intellect. One of his professors later wrote about him in the *Cambridge Review*:

> I had only a brief knowledge of John Cornford, but it will never pass from my memory […] His belief in Communism was no youthful effervescence; it was a still water which ran deep […] He had a first-rate mind; but he had also something greater – very much greater. He was one of those who are willing to stake heart's blood upon their convictions, turning them into a faith, and acting in the strength of their faith.[6]

3 Jon Clark, Margot Heinemann, David Margolies & Carol Snee, 'Louis MacNeice, John Cornford and Clive Branson: Three Left-Wing poets', in Jon Clark (ed.), *Culture and Crisis in Britain in the Thirties* (London: Lawrence & Wishart, 1979), p.116. I am grateful to Jane Bernal for drawing this to my attention.
4 Letter from John Cornford to Margot Heinemann, 21 November 1936, p.182 in the present volume.
5 Neal Wood, *Communism and British Intellectuals*, London: Victor Gollancz, 1959, p.55.
6 Professor Ernest Barker, *Cambridge Review*, 5 February 1937, cited in P. Sloan, *John Cornford: A Memoir*, p.252.

Today the name of John Cornford lives on in Spain. In the town of Lopera, scene of the bitter fighting in December 1936, lies *el Jardín del Pilar Viejo* (known also as the Garden of the English Poets). Within it stands a monument to Cornford and to his comrade Ralph Fox, both of whom were killed on the same day. And in April 2016, thanks to the work of A.A.B.I., there will be a ceremony at Lopera dedicated to Cornford, Fox and the other international volunteers who fought in the disastrous battle. There are also plans to install new plaques to the fallen at a number of other appropriate sites. Whether these will reach fruition or not, a memorial to Cornford and his fellow members of the English-speaking section of the 14th International Brigade will always remain: just to the east of the town lies a small hill that, eighty years later, locals still refer to as *la colina inglés*, the English hill, where these brave fighters for Spanish democracy fell.

Richard Baxell
November 2015

Political Change in the Writings
of John Cornford
by Jane Bernal

John Cornford was barely twenty-one when he was killed. The letters, poems and essays in this book are the work of a very young man who, because of his own personality and the extraordinary times he was living through, was learning fast and changing rapidly.

These days he is best known for his poetry, something that surprised his student contemporaries, many of whom did not even know that he wrote poems, let alone private, personal love poems. 'Sad Poem' was written as he was splitting up with his first serious girlfriend, Ray Peters, the mother of his son James Cornford. He wrote 'A Happy New Year' just after Christmas 1935, when he had to leave Ringstead Mill, where he had spent the holidays with his new love, Margot Heinemann. John did not want to leave, but he could not stay; he had to go to Cardiff as a delegate from the Federation of Student Societies to the University Labour Federation and she had to return to her work as a teacher in Birmingham.[1] 'A Happy New Year' does not appear in *John Cornford: A Memoir*,[2] the book of essays and poems published in 1938. In the back of Margot Heinemann's personal copy of that book she has written the poem out in ink, with the title *'Parting', RJC Unpublished*. John Cornford's most famous love poem is also addressed to Margot and is generally known, as it is in this volume, as 'To Margot Heinemann', though when it first appeared, in 1938, in *New Writing* it was simply called 'Poem'.[3]

---

1 P. Stansky & W. Abrahams, 'John Cornford - Cambridge', *Journey to the Frontier: Two Roads to the Spanish Civil War* (The Norton Library, 1983), p.243.
2 P. Sloan, *John Cornford: A Memoir* (London: Jonathan Cape; 1938).
3 J. Cornford, 'Poem', *New Writing*, 1937.

In the 1970s, following the original publication of *Understand the Weapon, Understand the Wound*, there was a revival of interest in John Cornford's poetry. Margot made notes of her memories of John for a BBC Open University programme, *A Poet and Politics*. 'He always looked a bit untidy though dignified – only partly from indifference to bourgeois standards – the other part was that he was always hard up, having only an allowance from his parents (out of which he had to meet heavy personal expenses) and not liking in the circumstances to ask them to increase it. His clothes were always a bit too small because he had gone on growing after he last bought any – he had a good tweed jacket of about the right size (inherited from Mike Straight), but his old jacket sleeves were too short & his trousers above his ankles. He had an aged green polo sweater and an aged navy shirt. I <u>once</u> saw him in a suit with a cloth tie (probably it was for his appearance in court, though I'm not sure), & that I think must have been a school suit & was <u>very</u> much too small. His hands & feet were very small for a tall man. He was strong and active, though slightly clumsy physically [...] He was terrifically energetic, enjoyed walking and outdoor things.'

'He had great personal charm,' she wrote – 'that's to say he was very shy and could be absolutely silent – but when interested lost his shyness and had a great deal to say – with great clarity and emphasis, speaking too fast and emphasising his points with a soaring hand gesture or with fist in palm [...] not loud-mouthed or liking sound of his own voice.' He was never an orator, nor obviously persuasive but thought deeply, and convinced people by his logic and knowledge. She describes him as very gentle and unwilling to hurt anyone, something that it is harder to infer from his writing.[4]

4   M. Heinemann, 'Some Notes (On John Cornford and Communist Party in Cambridge in the 1930s)', Goldsmiths College UoL, ed. Margot Heinemann Archive. Manuscript notes probably made in preparation for 'A Poet and Politics' for Open University ed: Special collections; Undated, probably 1977), p.3.

There are few contemporary accounts of John. Most, like Margot's 1970s manuscript, are coloured by knowing what happened next. As both Jonathan Galassi and Richard Baxell have pointed out, his short life has given rise to many contradictory myths. However his total conviction and commitment seems to have impressed people he met even briefly, for example the poet Louis MacNeice who once gave him a lift to Birmingham.[5] Even as a student he knew a lot, and was keen to learn more, about the British working-class and labour movement. He worked as a volunteer at the Labour Research Department when he was at LSE (London School of Economics). His work there was to explain the finances of the London Passenger Transport Board (forerunner of London Transport) to Trade Union branches and the busmen's Rank and File movement. Margot wrote that John was intensely interested in working people: 'not to analyse them sociologically, but in admiration of what kept their spirit and the movement going in the hardest times.' Margot, who was certainly no Maoist, thought that John would have 'wholeheartedly agreed with Chinese Communist's idea of sending all intellectuals to work in the villages and learn from the workers: he thought of it that way round, rather than his ability to teach them anything'.[6]

The historian Kevin Morgan, writing about middle-class recruits to Communism in the UK in the 1930s, points out that this was not a single generational cohort and that the Party that these young people joined was one that was changing rapidly over time. Relatively small differences in the time of joining the Party could often make a big difference in the sort of Party one joined.[7] James Klugmann, a close friend of John's, said in 1977

---

5 L. MacNeice, *The Strings Are False* (London: Faber & Faber; 1965, p.157). See also MacNeice's letter to Anthony Blunt on 7 May 1936 in J. Allison (ed.), *Letters of Louis MacNeice* (London: Faber & Faber; 2010), p.263.

6 M. Heinemann, 'Some Notes', *op. cit.*

7 K. Morgan, 'Recruiting the Middle-class' in N. Deakin (ed.), *Radiant Illusion?: Middle-Class recruits to Communism in the 1930s* (Kent: Eden Valley Editions, 2015), pp.67–87.

that 'There are some periods in history where things hardly move [...] and there are periods of extreme change, struggle and storm. The thirties was definitely such a stormy period.'[8] He argued that it was important to understand the Communist Party if you were to understand the decade. He saw it moving from 'an extraordinarily difficult period, a bad period if you like, at the end of the twenties and early thirties to an extremely fruitful period in the middle and later thirties – from 'Class against Class' to 'United Front' to 'Popular Front'.'

John Cornford's work is interesting for many reasons, but I think one of them is that his life in the Communist Party spanned a period of such rapid change. The 'Class against Class' period, when the official 'Line' required communists to describe the Labour Party as the third Capitalist Party or even as 'Social Fascists', to the Popular Front that attempted to unite the vast majority of people against war and fascism. Hitler's victory in Germany meant that communists internationally had to reconsider their strategy. By 1932, the Communist Party in Britain was already, and with some difficulty, pulling away from 'Class against Class' guidelines in its industrial work.[9] In 1935 the Seventh World Congress of the Communist International extended the idea of the Popular Front, of alliances and unity with Social Democratic parties, across all Communist parties. It was accepted and supported by Stalin in the end, but originated with Maurice Thorez – the leader of the French communists – and Georgi Dimitrov, the Bulgarian who was accused of starting the Reichstag fire and who conducted his own defence at the subsequent trial.

John was very well aware of the change; for example in 'Full Moon at Tierz', with its references to Maurice Thorez

---

8   J. Klugmann, 'Introduction: The Crisis in the Thirties: A View from the Left' in J. Clark, M. Heinemann, D. Margolies & C. Snee (eds), *Culture and Crisis in Britain in the 30s* (London: Lawrence & Wishart, 1979), pp.13-36.

9   N. Branson, 'Fascism and the United Front (1933–1935)', *The History of the Communist Party of Great Britain: 1927–1941* (London: Lawrence & Wishart; 1985), p.110.

and Dimitrov, 'Here what the Seventh Congress said, / If true, if false is live or dead'. His friends seem to have felt the same. In 1937 'a group of contemporaries' (who chose not to identify themselves individually but who certainly included Heinemann, Victor Kiernan, Klugmann and Bernard Knox) contributed a chapter on Cambridge Socialism to *John Cornford: A Memoir*. When they describe John as having been 'the most brilliant, the most sectarian, the most conspiratorial, the most devoted and full of animal energy, the most at times in need of a shave and a haircut', there is a sense that they are looking back affectionately into what they now see as a distant political past.[10] In 1932, Rajani Palme Dutt, who was the editor of *Labour Monthly* and a leading theoretician, stated that a communist intellectual should 'forget that he is an intellectual and (except in moments of necessary self-criticism) remember only that he is a Communist'. By 1934, thinking in the CP was shifting towards the Popular Front strategy that was to be confirmed in 1935 by the Seventh World Congress. When Willie Gallacher, who, like Dutt, was a member of the Central Committee, visited the Cambridge students in 1934, attitudes to intellectuals had also shifted. He was impressed by the size of the student branch but not by the affectedly grubby clothes, the swearing or the disregard for academic activity. He told them, 'We want people who are capable, who are good scientists, historians and teachers. It doesn't follow at all you will be good workers. We need you as you are: if you have a vocation it's pointless to run away to factories. One or two of you may become full-time revolutionaries, but this is a thing that only a few of you will be able to do. We want you to study and become good students.'[11]

John may well have hoped that he would be one of the

10 A Group of Contemporaries, 'Cambridge Socialism 1933–1936' in P. Sloan (ed.), *John Cornford: A Memoir* (London: Jonathan Cape, 1938), pp.97–115.
11 N. Branson, 'Professional Workers, Students and Intellectuals, 1932–39', *History of the Communist Party of Great Britain: 1927-1941* (London: Lawrence & Wishart, 1985).

full-time revolutionaries, but he was also an academically brilliant historian. It is clear, too, that he did not he see himself as a megaphone for a party-line decided in King Street or Moscow. He was contributing to, as well as transmitting, political thought.

Reading what John himself wrote, and how his thinking shifted, helps us to make sense of the rapidly changing times through which he lived. Early in the thirties, communist students wanted to break decisively with their own past, their families, even the student movement and become 'workers'. By the mid-thirties they were striving to become 'good students', engaging creatively as Marxists with intellectual matters. John's poem 'Org. Com. Discussion on Literature' (probably written early 1934) has no time for bourgeois culture or poetry, 'Webster's skull & Eliot's pen [...] All we've brought are our party cards / which are no bloody good for your bloody charades.' By 1935 he is writing a critique of the history-teaching at Cambridge that seems to accept that there should be a history syllabus, though it should be very different from the current one. In a letter to his mother in June 1936 he even admits to wanting to do further research into the social roots of the Elizabethan poets.

In 'Communism at the Universities' (published in 1936), John complains that the Labour Party has never made a serious attempt to win the middle-class into alliance with the Labour movement on the basis of their own interests, but that this is something the Communist Party is just beginning to do. He argues that a student 'does not have to be interested in politics to come face-to-face with one great reality. The existence of the Capitalist structure of society means that there is an ever-widening gap between the potentialities of science, technique, culture and education, and their actual application in the world today. [...] For example the medical student comes up against the fact that hundreds of children suffer every year from rickets [...]'. He goes on to talk about graduate unemployment and the detail of what is taught at Universities. He gives a critique of the content of courses in both economics and history. This essay seems to me to be entirely different in tone as well as content from 'Students – Not Scabs' (May, 1933) and 'The Class Front of Modern Art' (December, 1933), and I do not think this is only because he was addressing a different audience. Some of the change is no doubt a result of his growing up (few of us think exactly the same at twenty as we did at eighteen), but even John's early writings are so accomplished and thoughtful that it is, I think, appropriate to take the work as a measure by which to track the shifts not only in his personal development, but also those in the wider political environment.

Jane Bernal
January 2016

Notes

p. 3

R van R G. The quotation is from Robert [von Ranke] Graves's poem 'To Be Less Philosophical', published in his *Poems 1926–1930*, Heinemann, 1931. Like Cornford, Graves had attended Copthorne School. The poet exerted a strong influence on the young literary enthusiast; in an essay composed in Switzerland in August 1931, Cornford wrote:

> Graves's importance to the future of poetry lies more in the principles of his poetic theory and his application of them to his own poetry than in the value of the experience communicated by the poetry, which is often highly specialized. (The relationship between the importance to the future of poetry and the goodness of the poetry of T. S. Eliot and Robert Graves gives an interesting parallel to that between the poetry of Keats and Wordsworth. There are few, I think, who would seriously consider calling Wordsworth a 'better' poet than Keats or Graves a 'better' poet than Eliot. Yet Wordsworth had a very important and beneficial influence on the future of poetry and Keats a very bad influence indeed. For Keats's influence was confined to an imitation of his style and choice of subject matter among minor poets, while Wordsworth's lay in an acceptance of those principles which he applied to his own poetry. Similarly, to judge T. S. Eliot's influence on the future by that which he exercises over some contemporary poets, it seems confined to an imitation of the superficial qualities of his poetry, while those poets, few as they are, who have been seriously influenced by Graves, at least continue to keep an independence which T. S. Eliot's imitators entirely lack, and have probably gained more by an acceptance of some of his principles than they have lost by imitation of his language.
>
> [...] The importance of those principles which make Graves a poet of such great potential importance to the future of poetry is the principle of accuracy which he has emphasized in all his critical writings. [...]

p. 10

'At least to know the sun rising each morning'. Cornford sent this poem to his friend Tristan Jones in February 1932, writing:

> Here is my latest and I think my best poem. It is conceived as a sort of letter to Philip Gell, who stands in the same relation to me here as you used to and do when you are present. I don't know whether you can find any coherence in it. There is none intellectually, but I feel it as a whole, and hope you can find the connection too. I like, as they stand, I. and II. best, particularly I. They were actually written in the order II., III., I., IV.

p. 13

For Elisabeth. For a period, Cornford was romantically attached to Elisabeth Raverat, daughter of his mother's cousin, Gwen Raverat.

p. 16

Org. Com. Discussion on Literature. Margot Heinemann and others called this poem 'Keep Culture Out of Cambridge', and the name stuck. Its original title, and the word 'obscure', which was printed 'obscene' in Pat Sloan's book, are restored here.
Org. Com. Organizing Committee.

p. 17

Unaware was published in *The Listener*, 25 April 1934, under the pseudonym of Dai Barton.
As Our Might Lessens. The first three sections appeared in *New Writing 4*, autumn 1937. Section 2 was also published as 'Poem' in the Penguin *New Writing 10*, edited by John Lehmann, November 1941.

p. 21

Sergei Mironovitch Kirov. Kirov (1886-1924), a leading early Bolshevik, head of the Communist Party in Leningrad, was assassinated in December 1934. It is now believed that Stalin, jealous of Kirov's influence in the Party, was responsible and used his death as a pretext for the repression of dissident Old Bolshevik elements in the party.

p. 22

A Happy New Year. A typescript version of this poem bears the notation, '3.1.36 Cardiff'.

p. 23
Full Moon at Tierz: Before the Storming of Huesca first appeared in the *Left Review*, March 1937.

p. 25
To Margot Heinemann, as it is called here, was first published as 'Poem' in *New Writing 4*, autumn 1937. Under the title 'Huesca', it came out in the Penguin *New Writing 2*, January 1941.

p. 26. *A Letter from Aragon* was printed in the *Left Review*, November 1936. It also appeared in *The Cambridge Review*, 5 February 1937. *H. E.* High Explosives.

p. 31
Students – Not Scabs was published in *The Student Vanguard*, I, 5, May 1933.

p. 32
Art and the Class-Struggle: A Reply to Rayner Heppenstall was printed in *The Student Vanguard*, May 1933, in response to Rayner Heppenstall's article 'T. S. Eliot – Sign of the Times', published in the March 1933 issue.

p. 34
The Class Front of Modern Art appeared in *The Student Vanguard*, II, 3, December 1933.

p. 39
Julian Bell and John Cornford on Art. Bell's response to 'The Class Front of Modern Art', together with Cornford's comment, came out in the January 1934 issue of *The Student Vanguard* (II, 4). A further rejoinder by Bell, published in *The Student Vanguard* (II, 6), in March 1934, reads as follows:

> I don't want to prolong this controversy unduly, but I feel that I must make a protest against Comrade Cornford's attribution to me of the opinions of Mr. Leavis. What he calls an objective restatement of my case is in part a repetition of points of fact about the present intellectual situation, as to which we are agreed, in part, an attempt to show that I approve of that situation, which I do not.

I attempted to show: (1) That it is almost impossible in England to-day for anyone to write poetry that will be read by the present English working class; (2) That the younger revolutionary poets are in fact simply writing romantic-subjective poetry about their revolutionary feelings; (3) That this is not a particularly useful activity from the point of view of anyone wishing to bring about a revolution; (4) That it should be possible to write prose that would be directly useful and that would be read by the working class.

A further point that should be made is that there is no reason to suppose that the poetry written at present by romantic revolutionaries is likely to be judged more valuable in some future socialist state than the poetry at present being written by romantic reactionaries. To assert that the arts are conditioned by the forms of society, or to prophesy the appearance of a great age of literature as a result of successful socialist revolution is one thing; it is quite another to infer a peculiar merit as poetry (or as propaganda) in the work of socialist writers. In the one case there is a profound and all-embracing long-period change; in the other a personal conversion.

How many of our 'revolutionary' poets can be trusted not to turn Fascist?

p. 45
Left? appeared in *Cambridge Left*, winter 1933–4.

p. 51
The Struggle for Power in Western Europe was published in *Cambridge Left*, spring 1934.

p. 63
Notes on the Teaching of History at Cambridge was first published in Pat Sloan's *John Cornford: A Memoir*.

p. 69
What Communism Stands For was written for inclusion in a symposium entitled *Christianity and the Social Revolution*, edited by John Lewis, Karl Polanyi and Donald K. Kitchin, and published by Victor Gollancz in 1935. Other contributors included W. H. Auden, John Macmurray, Joseph Needham and Roy Pascal.

p. 92

Communism in the Universities appeared in *Young Minds for Old: Fourteen Young University Writers on Modern Problems*, edited by Lincoln Ralphs, published by Frederick Muller in 1936.

p. 100

The Situation in Catalonia. Portions of this essay, with slight revisions in paragraphing and phraseology, were printed in *The New Republic*, 2 December 1936, under the title 'On the Catalonian Front'.

p. 107

C.A.D.C.I. Centre Autonomista de Dependents del Comerç i de la Indústria.

p. 122

At the bottom of this letter a note in Frances Cornford's hand says, 'J. just sent me his poetry as by "a boy at Stowe" for criticism. *Don't* let on to the outside world that he writes it – or he'll *never* forgive me!'

p. 123

Reg. One of Christopher Cornford's masters at Stowe, Reginald Snell became a close friend of the entire Cornford family.

p. 124

a song about tapestry. 'Tapestry Song' was published in *Mountains and Molehills* by the Cambridge University Press in 1934.

p. 125

Uncle Bernard. Bernard Darwin, 1876–1961, golf critic of *The Times* and *Country Life*, was Frances Cornford's half-brother.
JHAS. John Hanbury Angus Sparrow, 1906–1992, Fellow and later Warden of All Souls College, Oxford.

p. 126

Part of this letter has been lost.
CRS. Cyril Spencer, one of Cornford's masters at Stowe.
CFC. Christopher Francis Cornford, 1917–1993, John's younger brother, was at this point also at Stowe.
GMT. George Macaulay Trevelyan, 1876–1962, historian.

p. 127
Helena. Helena Darwin Cornford Henderson, 1913–1996, John's elder sister.
Middleton M. John Middleton Murry, 1889–1957, journalist and critic, founder and editor of *The Adelphi*, 1923–48.

p. 129
WdLM. Walter de la Mare, 1873–1956, poet.
William. William of Orange, about whom Helena was then writing an essay.

p. 130
This letter and the poem included in it are partly lost. The poem is probably the 'Alcibiades' referred to in Cornford's letter of 28 February 1931.

p. 131
Richard Hughes. Novelist and poet, 1900–76, author of *A High Wind in Jamaica*.

p. 132
Sidney Schiff. (1868–1944), a friend of Frances Cornford, and the author, under the pen-name Stephen Hudson, of a number of novels; he also translated the last volume of Proust. He met Cornford in Switzerland during the winter of 1931–2, and was immediately impressed with him. In a letter of 16 April 1932, he wrote to Frances Cornford:

> Certainly John is too intellectual and within my small means, I endeavour and shall endeavour to distract his mind towards merely human preoccupations. But spirit is not susceptible to restraint or to deflection when it has established so complete an autonomy as John's has. The austerity of his intellect is quite outside of my experience of youth and the only naiveté I have so far perceived in him is in his apparent unconsciousness of his own apartness and in his ignorance of (innocence) the limits of his own consciousness. Temperamentally and morally he seems to me to be antithetic to Billy or it would be truer to say that they are complementary in that context. Intellectually they are clever; there is, I think, affinity between them but, of course, Billy's mind is quite untrained and

all he knows has been acquired almost haphazard. But he is in the highest degree sensitive and intuitively he will reach, has already reached, truths unknown to John (and to all but a few of those older than himself) which enable him to form an empirical judgment about things he has little or no knowledge of. John's chief defects are his certainty and distrust. Both have come about through his having been obliged to accept the company of his intellectual inferiors and the conventions he disdains. He has learnt early that most men are fools and liars. I have asked him to let me have a copy in type of his poems before I see him on the 22nd when we expect him to lunch and I hope, to spend the afternoon with me.

p. 133
CH. Conduit Head, the Cornfords' home in Cambridge.
Heckstall Smith. A mathematics master at Stowe.

p. 134
FMC. Francis Macdonald Cornford, John's father.

p. 136
the Hugh Stewarts. Hugh Stewart, chaplain of Trinity, was an authority on Pascal. His wife Jesse Stewart was the biographer of Francis Cornford's mentor Jane Ellen Harrison.

p. 138
Esther. Esther Polianowsky Salaman, 1900–1995, physicist and novelist, was a close friend of Frances Cornford.

p. 140
McGreevy. Thomas MacGreevy, 1893–1967, poet and critic, author of *T. S. Eliot: A Study*, Chatto & Windus, 1931.

p. 145
Joe Henderson. 1903–2007, psychiatrist, an American student of Jung, who later married Helena Cornford. He contributed the chapter 'Ancient Myths and Modern Man' to Jung's *Man and His Symbols*.

p. 146
I.C.I. Imperial Chemical Industries.

pp. 148–9
The placement of these letters, and of others in this selection that are undated, is conjectural.

p. 154
that foreign Ll. G. David Lloyd George, 1863–1945, whose father was Welsh.

p. 155
Alan Barlow. Sir James Alan Barlow, 1881–1968, Principal Assistant Secretary, Ministry of Labour, 1931–4. Private Secretary to Ramsay MacDonald, 1932–1934. He was married to Nora Darwin, 1885–1989, a cousin of Frances Cornford.

p. 157
Here they all are. See p. 150.

p. 159
FCC. Frances Crofts Cornford, John's mother.
RPD. Rajani Palme Dutt (1882-1957), leading political theorist and journalist for the Communist Party of Great Britain.

p. 161
SS LP. Socialist Society, Labour Party.

p. 161
To Frances Cornford [1932/3]. Written on a visit to the Alan Barlows. See Frances Cornford's letter on p. 154.
the Keynes's. Margaret Darwin, 1890–1974, a cousin of Frances Cornford, was married to Sir Geoffrey Keynes, 1887–1982, the physician and editor of Blake.
W. Lewis. Percy Wyndham Lewis, 1882–1957, whose novel *The Apes of God* (1930) contained a chapter, 'Chez Lionel Kein, Esq.', which satirized the Schiffs.

p. 162
To Tristan Jones [Spring 1933]. Written during Cornford's period in London between Stowe and Cambridge, when he was enrolled at the London School of Economics.
Nanking. A Chinese restaurant.

FSS. Federation of Student Societies.
Vanguard. The Student Vanguard.
L.R.D. Group. Labour Research Department Group on the economics of transport industries.

p. 163
S of F. South of France.

p. 164
Catriona. A novel by Robert Louis Stevenson, published in 1893.
Y.C.L. Young Communist League.

p. 166
Inprecorr. International Press Correspondence, weekly news-sheet of the 3rd International.

p. 167
I.L.P. Independent Labour Party, a left-wing offshoot of the Labour Party, one of whose leaders was James Maxton.
C.P.G.B. Communist Party of Great Britain.
N.C.L.C. National Council of Labour Colleges.

p. 168
Justin. Justin Brooke, a friend of the elder Cornfords, owned a fruit farm in Suffolk.

p. 169
Richard. Richard Bennett, b. 1912, a journalist, went with Cornford to Spain and worked in radio in Barcelona. He served in the Army Bureau of Current Affairs in the Second World War, and later edited *Lilliput* (1946–50) and wrote for *The Sunday Telegraph*.

p. 170
CNT. Confederación Nacional del Trabajo.
E.R.C. Esquerra Republicana de Catalunya.
UGT. Unión General de Trabajadores.

p. 178
C.I. Communist International.

p. 183
Bernard. Bernard M.W. Knox, 1914–2010, a fellow-student and political activist with Cornford at Trinity, later a classical scholar in the USA.

Index